Eld. R. H. Miller.

# The Life of
# Elder R. H. Miller

BY

**Otho Winger, A. M.**
Professor of History and Philosophy
in Manchester College

ELGIN, ILLINOIS
BRETHREN PUBLISHING HOUSE.
1910

Copyright 1910
Brethren Publishing House
Elgin, Illinois

To the
Church of the Brethren,
for whose welfare the subject of this
biographical sketch gave a life
of faithful service,
This Work is Dedicated

# BIBLIOGRAPHY

Church Periodicals, on file at Brethren's Publishing House, Elgin, Ill.

Full Reports of Annual Meeting since 1876.

Classified Minutes of Annual Meeting, compiled by S. S. Mohler.

Brethren's Family Almanac.

Record of the Faithful, by Howard Miller.

The Brethren's Reasons.

History of the Tunkers and the Brethren Church, by H. R. Holsinger.

Two Centuries of the Church of the Brethren.

Life of John Kline, by Benjamin Funk.

Life and Sermons of Elder James Quinter, by Mary N. Quinter.

Life of Uncle John Metzger, by M. M. Eshelman.

## CONTENTS

| | | | Page |
|---|---|---|---|
| Chapter | I. | Early Life and Ministry | 16 |
| Chapter | II. | Debates | 27 |
| Chapter | III. | Editorial Work | 41 |
| Chapter | IV. | Selections from Editorials | 51 |
| Chapter | V. | Educational Work | 83 |
| Chapter | VI. | Division | 94 |
| Chapter | VII. | Annual Meeting | 123 |
| Chapter | VIII. | A Preacher of the Gospel | 140 |
| Chapter | IX. | Selected Sermons | 150 |
| Chapter | X. | Later Life and Death | 219 |
| Chapter | XI. | Contemporaries | 237 |

# INTRODUCTION.

THE biographies of great and good men who have lived for principle and have been as true as steel to their convictions of right, regardless of consequences, are the rich heritage of the present and the future. The very best legacy a man can leave to posterity is the heritage of a pure life, a good name and duty well and faithfully done, and it is our duty to see that such names and such men are not forgotten. To forget our leaders in thought and action is to lose one of the strongest assets of Church or State. A great man of the State has said: "When people cast aside sentiments of patriotism and ideals of loyalty they become sordid, and sordidness marches hand in hand with vice." So when the Church casts aside sentiments of love and reverence, forgetting her good men of the past, she grows indifferent and indifference begets disintegration and loss of unity. We need to be taught to revere the memories of those who have faithfully fought the fight of faith and have stood unflinchingly for the right as God gave them to see the right.

Our land is dotted with monuments in recognition of the services of the heroes of war and peace, who have unselfishly given their lives to the services of their country, and our libraries are teeming with biographies, volume crowding volume, setting forth heroic deeds and virtues. If it is needful that the State, in this way, has occasion to teach patience and loyalty, why should not the Church also teach sentiments of loyalty to Christ in the same way? The memories of our faithful leaders, their self-sacrifice, their devotion to principle and their example of faithfulness, will be a great help to us who are left to fight the battles in our own days. We have not hasted to give recognition to the good qualities of the fathers, for only in recent years has biography become a recognized fact in our church literature.

And so we gladly welcome the biography of one of our great leaders of the Church, a man who left a deep impress upon her work during the last half of the nineteenth century, a man who had the courage of his convictions, a man faithful to Christ and the Church, a man of strong mentality, a leader among men, a wise counsellor, the logician and debater, a mighty man of God who fell in harness doing valiant battle for the truth, Elder Robert H. Miller.

The author has done his work well and those who read his book will appreciate the labor of love that has preserved to us, in endurable form, the life and labor of one of our great men. In every home in our Brotherhood this book should find a hearty welcome. It will be read with deep and abiding interest and the reading will be helpful. Added value is given to the book because the author has wisely included short biographical sketches of a number of Brother Miller's colaborers. He has also rescued from oblivion a number of the best sermons, editorials and speeches coming from the active brain of Brother Robert, as he was called by his colaborers and by those who knew him best and loved him most.

# INTRODUCTION

No word of the writer of this introduction can add value to the biography of our beloved brother. The author has done his part with conscientious fidelity and with a high motive. He has written and written well. May God bless the work thus performed and make it a blessing to the Church and to humanity.

D. L. MILLER.

## PREFACE.

It was Carlyle who said that the history of the world is the biographies of great men. In one respect, this is true of the Church. This institution today is largely what influential men have made it. To know the history of these men is to know much of the history of the Church. The Church of the Brethren has produced great men; not great in the eyes of the world, but in depth of soul, largeness of heart, breadth of intellect and sincere devotion to a noble cause, they are the peers of many whose names are prominent in the pages of history. The author believes that to know more of these men and their labors will create a greater love for the church, and fire the heart with zeal for better service. It was this conviction that prompted the undertaking of this work, which records the life and services of one of the most valiant of God's children.

Our church fathers showed in many ways their intense love for the church. No sacrifice was too great for them to make, if only they could be of use to the Master. They did not go as foreign missionaries, but their work at home proved that they had the true missionary spirit. Not only did they give their means, but they gave themselves. Though the churches failed to do their duty in supporting them in a financial way, yet they did not falter. Their interest in perishing souls was too great to permit them to wait until they were paid for their services. They cared little for worldly honor. They thought only of preserving the church in its purity and truth, keeping it free from the vanities and evils of the world. To the careless observer, their work may seem insignificant; but a more careful study of their lives forces the conviction that the present generation must bestir itself or it will not accomplish as much of real value for the church as did our fathers. They have handed down to us a precious heritage, which we should improve and pass on to succeeding generations.

No claim is made to original knowledge concerning the facts in this volume. The work has been written from data gleaned in many fields. On another page is found a bibliography of books used. Many persons have kindly furnished important information. Acknowledgment of help is made where convenient to do so; but I owe thanks to many whose names cannot be mentioned, because the list of those that I have consulted is too long. Special mention, however, should be made of help received from Elders S. S. Ulrey and L. W. Teeter and D. L. Miller. The latter two have read the manuscript and offered corrections and appropriate suggestions. Sister R. H. Miller has gladly furnished me with manuscripts and papers that Brother Robert left in his own handwriting. The work is now sent forth with the hope that it will prove a useful addition to our church literature.

OTHO WINGER.

*North Manchester, Ind., Sept., 1909.*

## CHAPTER I.

### Early Life and Ministry.

Many citizens of Indiana and Illinois trace the westward movement of their ancestors from Virginia or the Carolinas to Kentucky, and in turn from this pioneer transallegheny State to more promising lands lying beyond the Ohio River. This movement began in the last quarter of the eighteenth century and continued for more than fifty years. These early settlers generally came in bands, but often single families would lead the way to unknown regions. They generally stopped in Kentucky for a few years before moving on. They became small landholders but, as a rule, they were neither ambitious nor thrifty. They were not seeking for riches but for homes. They were men and women of strong will, adventurous spirit, and virile character. They were often rude in manners and manifested little interest in education. They showed a marked individuality and a great love of freedom. They possessed unquestioned patriotism and frequently intense religious zeal, though they were generally narrow in their views of religious toleration. From these pioneers have descended a class of citizens whom the nation now honors among her noblest children; and among these is included the name of the subject of this biography.

Robert Henry Miller was born in Shelby County, Ky., June 7, 1825. His father, Robert Miller, was a

## EARLY LIFE AND MINISTRY

native of Rockbridge County, Va. When a young man he emigrated to Shelby County, Ky., where he married Miss Mary Blaydes. To them eight children were born, of whom Robert H. was the second. The parents were poor and when Robert was seven years old they moved to Montgomery County, Ind., and settled near Ladoga. The country was then new and the educational advantages were few. In the old log schoolhouses, for which Indiana has become famous in literature, Robert enjoyed for a few months each year the meagre educational advantages in those days. He was quiet and studious, and during vacation he would rather take his books and spend a day in the woods in deep meditation than to play with other boys.

From a boy he took great delight in debating and was always noted for the force of the arguments he brought to bear upon the proposition he undertook to prove. Though naturally timid, his opponent in debate could never intimidate him and drive him from his position. One of his early debates was with Oliver Wilson on the question of capital punishment, which Robert opposed. One who was present tells of the interest aroused in the neighborhoood over this debate and says, " No difference how strong the arguments Ol Wilson would bring forward, Bob Miller was ready to uproot them."

These early debates, held in the country schoolhouses when Robert was yet in his teens, were unconsciously preparing him for the discussion of greater questions in after years. He also took an active part in a mock legislature that continued for a long time. Here he showed ability that would likely have manifested itself at a later date in the State or National Congress, had not the Master called him to the higher and nobler work of the ministry.

In his early years his voice was not good, but he made successful efforts to control it. He was awkward in gait, and also in manner when before an audience. He was a ready wit and often put his antagonist to a decided disadvantage in repartee. Among his young men associates he had no enemies, and was frequently the leader in many of their sports.

After careful study at home, he attended the Waveland (Indiana) Academy, a Presbyterian school for the preparation of teachers. How long he attended this school is not definitely known, but he probably completed the course that was then offered. He afterwards studied law, but never regularly practiced at the bar; though he was engaged in minor cases and was called in the language of those days, " a pettifogger." He early came in demand as a temperance speaker and as such was well known in his own and surrounding neighborhoods. He also took some part in political campaigns.

He taught two terms of school. This was in a typical Indiana schoolhouse of that day: A log structure with stick chimney, slab benches, poor light, few books and very little of the comfort of the schoolhouse of later years. The students took their exercise by going to the forest and cutting their own firewood. Elder W. R. Harshbarger, who still lives at Ladoga, Ind., and a brother-in-law to Robert, was one of the small boys in that school.

The strong and unbending character, that was so

## EARLY LIFE AND MINISTRY 19

well known in later life, persistently manifested itself from youth. His brother says, " I never knew him to swear an oath nor use any vulgar language in his boyhood days. The wicked, wild, young men were no company for him." At the age of nineteen be became intensely interested in a Methodist camp meeting held near Waveland. There seems to be some uncertainty as to whether he was really converted at this time, but whatever change of heart there was it was kept from his father; for since the latter was a strong Baptist, and much opposed to the Methodists, Robert did not want to wound his father's feelings.

At any rate he did not join the Methodists nor any other denomination until he was thirty-three years old. He was married to Sarah C. Harshbarger, November 19, 1846. She was two years his junior and was the daughter of Samuel Harshbarger, a deacon in the German Baptist Brethren church. It was largely her influence that caused him to become interested in the church for which he was to give the best years of his life. This, however, did not occur until twelve years later. During most of this time he was engaged in farming. He occasionally invested in stock, but in this he seems to have been unsuccessful. A growing family, sickness and the deaths of two of his children increased his financial difficulties.

The real history of Robert H. Miller began when he united with the church in 1858. It is evident that ever since his marriage he had been more or less inclined toward the Church of the Brethren. He had been reading his Bible and had frequent discussions with William Byrd, a Universalist. Elder Elias Caylor, of

Hamilton County, had been invited by the Ladoga brethren to come and hold a few meetings in that congregation. Some of them believed that the time was at hand for an ingathering. Elder Caylor came and Robert and his wife made application for membership and were baptized.

The old brethren were not slow to put such promising talent to work. Six months later an election was held in the Raccoon congregation for two ministers. The old church papers show that the election was held August 16, 1858. They read as follows: " Election held in the Raccoon church for two ministers; R. H. Miller and Daniel Stoner were made the choice of the church." This was signed by Hiel Hamilton, Matthias Frantz, Daniel Himes and Wesley Burkett. The vote further shows that Brother Robert received the vote of every member of the church.

Brother Robert accepted the office with the determination to prove himself a workman that needeth not be ashamed. Whatever of law practice or political speaking he had been engaged in was now given up that he might devote himself to his nobler calling. He preached well from the first and very soon became the leading preacher of the Brethren in that part of the State. His advancement to the second degree, and ordination to the eldership followed in rapid succession. The exact dates of his advancement are not known, inasmuch as these papers, with many others of value, were burned with his house in 1863. By this time, however, he was elder in charge of his home congregation and remained its faithful shepherd for twenty years.

During all this time he was becoming better and

## EARLY LIFE AND MINISTRY 21

better known, first in Southern Indiana, and then throughout the Brotherhood, until his name was familiar to nearly every member of the church. The first man that he baptized was Wilson Spaulding, of Little Walnut, Putnam County, Ind. At dinner, after the baptism, Brother Robert said that he felt that he was doing some good by converting one man. Thereupon Brother Spaulding at once corrected him by saying that it was not Robert Miller but Daniel Miller, an old minister who had long had great influence over him.

He attended his first Annual Meeting at Hagerstown, Ind., in 1864. This was the last meeting for Elder John Kline, who was moderator that year, and who was cruelly murdered shortly after his return to Virginia. How fitting is the arrangement of the Master, that as one veteran lays down the cross, another is raised up to bear it forward. Brother Robert, on returning home, said that he did not make a speech because there were so many brethren there more able than he was.

Then, too, the old brethren looked with distrust upon a young man who dared to be too forward. In later years Brother Robert related the following incident taken from his early experience: " I remember once when young in the ministry, in company with another young preacher at Annual Meeting, we understood it was announced for us to preach in a town near by. When we had taken our seats a number of old ministers came into the crowded house. As we were young and strangers to nearly all, our embarrassment was like a load; still we hoped it would wear away. But just at the time for opening services, an old brother came to us and said we were out of our place and that we must give the stand to the old brethren. We told him that it had been announced for us, but he said, ' This belongs to Annual Meeting and you must give up to the old brethren.' I then said to the young brother with me that it was probable we would live to preach when these old brethren were gone, and we went down but not out. We resolved that if we would live and God would help, the time would come when they would not want us to go down."

Shortly before the Hagerstown meeting, Brother Robert had preached in that congregation at a regular service. Here he attracted much notice by his powerful preaching, which seemed all the more strange in those days that a *young* man of forty could have such power. One of brother Robert's attentive and admiring hearers was a young man, not yet a member of the church, but who was afterwards to become so well known as Elder Lewis W. Teeter, of Hagerstown, Ind. He says he was simply carried away by Brother Robert's pleasing style of speaking, and by the resistless force of his logical arguments.

From now on the years were busy ones. He was engaged in farming to earn a livelihood for his family; but he never neglected his church work. Whenever he had any time to spare he was with his books and hard at study. He began to uphold the doctrine of the Brethren in public debates, and continued to do so until he became one of the greatest religious debaters in the United States. His work in the Brotherhood at large began in 1869, when he first appeared on the Standing Committee at Annual Meeting. His influence on this body was soon felt and for twenty years no man was more effective in shaping the policies of the church. Another busy field was opened up in committee work. In this he was especially strong and was sent by Annual Meeting to all parts of the Brotherhood. Nor was this the extent of his labors, but realizing the need of a written work defending the doctrine of the church, he undertook and successfully completed, in 1876, his one great book, " The Doctrine of the Brethren Defended." For more than thirty years it has remained the standard work among the brethren in defense of their beloved principles.

For the church periodicals, at times, he was very active with the pen. The discussion of troublesome questions was often referred to him by the editors. He also had a large correspondence with brethren who sought his advice privately. His work in his home congregation and adjoining congregations did not slacken. Frequently he was called quite a distance by a local church that desired his help. On these trips he would sometimes spend many days, visiting several places, preaching strong, stirring sermons and building up the membership in the faith of the Gospel.

During these years he looked upon sorrow, sickness and death. His own health was often such that he was confined to his home for long periods, unable to attend to his pressing duties. Of the eight children born to his first union, the two oldest, a son and a daughter, died when quite small. His second son, John H., died Sept. 4, 1877, at the age of 22, after an illness of nearly two years. He had been Brother Robert's main help in running the farm, and his loss added new difficulties as well as great sorrow. Elder James Quinter officiated at his funeral. His third daughter, Sarah Jane, died of consumption, Feb. 1, 1880. At this time he wrote Elder Quinter: " To give up such children is full of hope for the spirit world, but oh, how sad and gloomy it leaves the dying objects of this, until nothing seems dear unless it has death or God or heaven ringing in it. Under these sorrows our pathway must be lonely and we can only look beyond the cold river made dearer because Jesus and Janie have passed through its waters."

But his cup of sorrow was not yet full. So much sickness brought him great expense. Being absent from home a great deal, his farm work was entrusted to others. For these reasons he failed financially and was forced to make an assignment. Nearly all of his creditors realized the cause of his misfortune and freely forgave him all the debt that he could not pay. The loss of their home, however, greatly weighed upon his wife. This, together with the late loss of their children, was greater than she could bear. Her health began to fail and in March, 1880, while Brother Robert was absent, she was stricken with pneumonia. He was hastily summoned to her bedside where he realized that the greatest sorrow of his life had come. His own account in the *Primitive Christian,* two weeks later, tells the sad story:

" Sarah C. Miller, wife of Elder R. H. Miller, died of pneumonia, March 26, 1880, aged 53 years, 1 month and 10 days. She was the daughter of Samuel Harshbarger, born in Botetout County, Va., and came to Indiana in her eleventh year. She leaves four children, two grandchildren, two sisters, five brothers and many friends to mourn a loss which all things of earth cannot supply. She was a faithful member of the church for over twenty years, a faithful wife and mother, though for most of her life she was in feeble health. She never ceased to overtax her strength until her work on earth was done. Long watching in weariness over her two children, who died of consumption, had so worn out her strength that she was unable to bear the severe attack of the disease by which she is called to lay down the cross and take up the crown.

"This is another deeper sorrow still added to our load of troubles. Wave after wave comes rolling over us, leaving a desolate home without a mother, while we weep in sorrow which no tongue or pen have language to tell. Every silent object around us brings back in sadness the fond memories of a wife and mother, a grown son and daughter, all taken in a little over two years. So soon have come these troubles, deep and lasting, that life and death seem mingled together, all earthly objects seem changed, and cares multiplied till with aching heart we turn to God and sympathizing friends for strength and help to bear the clouds and storms. We turn to him who is the Immanuel to lead us through the deep waters, sustained and better prepared to meet those that have gone before to the spirit land. All the interest of parental care turns us to the welfare of the children left with us that God may lead them up in faith and hope to follow the example of a Christian mother whose love and life has all been given for their good, that this weeping, dying family of earth may be a loving, rejoicing family in heaven."

The many letters of condolence which Brother Robert received at this time showed the high esteem in which he was held by the Brotherhood at large. The heavy hand of affliction seems only to have stirred him up to greater diligence in the Master's cause. The Annual Meeting of this year placed upon him more committee work than was ever placed upon any other brother in one year in the history of the church. The whole summer was given to these duties. In July of this year he accepted the presidency of Ashland College and in September he left the scenes of his life for nearly fifty years to enter larger fields of influence and service.

## CHAPTER II.

### DEBATES.

A debate between two men representing different denominations, on questions that pertain to their respective principles, was no uncommon thing during the nineteenth century. It has been claimed by some that these debates grew out of a narrow-minded, bigoted and intolerant religious zeal that cared more for humiliating an opponent than to find the exact truth of God's Word. But this view is evidently far from the truth, in a great many cases at least. Men of different denominations had strong convictions as to the teaching of the Bible on doctrinal subjects. Once convinced of the truth, they uncompromisingly advocated those principles and felt it to be their duty to bring others to the true light. Nothing that God's Word contains seemed small or trivial to them. In striking contrast to them is the preacher of the twentieth century, who advocates a liberal theology and who has no time nor inclination to stand up and defend many things which he considers trivial.

The Church of the Brethren has produced many able defenders of her principles. Because of the fact that she professes to accept the whole Bible and reject none, she has had many zealous opponents who have attempted to tear down her strongholds. Such a task is no easy undertaking in the face of a "Thus saith the Lord."

One of the earliest debaters in the Church of the Brethren was Elder George Wolfe, of Illinois. One of his debates was with a Catholic priest in the town of Kaskaskia, Ill. It was attended by the Governor of the State, who afterwards said that the arguments of Elder Wolfe against Catholicism were crushing. Elder D. B. Sturgis, of Illinois, also held a number of debates, one of which was with a Mormon elder. The next debater of much experience was Elder James Quinter. About 1853 he engaged in a debate on the subject of baptism with a Lutheran minister. Other debates followed from time to time. From September 1866 to September 1869 he engaged in six public discussions. Two of these debates were with ministers of the Lutheran church in Indiana on the subject of baptism. Three of them were held with ministers of the Disciple church, on the subjects of trine immersion, feet-washing, the Lord's supper and the salutation of the holy kiss. Of these, the one held with Elder McConnell, in Linn County, Iowa, was published in book form and had a large circulation in the Brotherhood. Elder Quinter did not greatly enjoy a debate and only engaged in them because he was urged repeatedly to do so. Then, too, he had such conviction of the truth of the position of the Church of the Brethren, and had such ability to defend those principles, that his brethren felt they had no one else to whom they could look. That his active work so suddenly stopped can largely be explained by the fact that another giant had appeared to whom the work of a debate was more pleasant; and to him Elder Quinter gladly gave the polemical defense of our principles. This man was Elder

R. H. Miller, the greatest debater that the Church of the Brethren has ever produced.

It has already been shown that Brother Robert was a debater from his boyhood days; and it was no unnatural thing that he should fall into this kind of work as soon as he began to uphold the principles of the church. His first religious debate was held near Greencastle, Indiana, in the spring of 1861, with Nathan Wright, a minister of the Disciple church. This early debate left its impression on the minds of the people, who still remember Brother Robert with the kindest of feelings.

His second debate was a greater task. It was held in February, 1869, in Howard County, Ind., with Elder B. M. Blount, a Disciple minister. Forty years afterward Elder Blount gives the following account of the origin of the debate: " The way the discussion came about, was that while I was preaching in that community I had preached a discourse on the subject of feet-washing. This created some comment in the neighborhood. Afterward Brother Miller preached several discourses in the same community and our brethren thought he did not properly represent our views. Hence he was asked if he would debate these differences; on replying in the affirmative, the matter was submitted to me. A correspondence followed ultimating in the wordy battle."

The debate lasted five days, and the following propositions were discussed, of which the first three were affirmed by Brother Robert and the last one by Elder Blount;

1. Scriptures teach that to dip a penitent believer

in water three times, face forward, is scriptural and valid baptism.

2. The Scriptures teach that feet-washing is an ordinance to be observed in the church.

3. The Scriptures teach the salutation of the holy kiss is to be observed as it is done by the Brethren, commonly called Dunkards.

4. The Scriptures teach that the bread and wine, taken in communion, at any hour of the day, on the first day of the week only, is the Lord's Supper.

Elder Blount further characterizes Brother Robert as a debater: "Robert Miller was a pleasant man to debate with. Sometimes he would indulge in personalities, but it may be he had reasons for it. I have no doubt that he was a sincere and honest man although, as I think, very much mistaken on the propositions discussed."

In March, 1872, Brother Robert held a debate with Elder Jewell, of the Disciple church, in Hamilton County, Ind. It lasted five days, and all the questions pertaining to the differences between the Brethren and the Disciples were discussed. A little incident occurred during this debate that showed Brother Robert's good memory. Elder Jewell read a passage from a history of baptism. Brother Robert claimed he did not read it all, and desired Elder Jewell to give him the book. The former refused, whereupon Brother Robert quoted at length from memory from the same work, not only what Elder Jewell had read but what he had not read. The next day after this debate closed there were four accessions to the Stony Branch church, and a number shortly after.

The next year he went to Southern Illinois to engage in a debate. What his experience was there is told by Elder J. H. Moore, to whom Brother Robert related the whole affair:

"As a debater, he had some unique experiences. About 1873 the Brethren secured his services for a discussion in a town some distance from the railroad. His reputation as an able preacher and a fine debater had gone before him, so on the day for his arrival at the railroad station, where one of the brethren was to meet him and convey him to the place of discussion, a number of boys from the town made it a point to be at the depot in time to get a first glimpse of the famous preacher. Brother Miller was naturally a fine looking man. When he alighted from the train and was greeted by the brother who came to meet him the boys scrutinized him with intense interest. In all their experiences they had never seen such a fine and intelligent looking man.

"A large trunk was unloaded from the train and taken possession of by Bro. Miller and the brother who had come to meet him. The trunk put the boys to surmising, and they soon decided that it was full of books. So, without waiting for further developments, they mounted their horses and returned to their town in all possible haste, and told everybody they met that they had seen the great debater, that he was a fine looking man, that he had a big trunk full of books, and was reading Greek, Hebrew and Latin all the time. Before Brother Miller reached the town, everybody knew of his coming, the boys had spread the news everywhere and the excitement was simply intense.

"The stir made by the boys so affected public sentiment and the man Brother Miller was to have met in debate, that the discussion actually fell through with and never came off. His opponent could not be induced to accept clearly-defined propositions, and so there was no debate. Brother Miller used to tell in an amusing way, how the boys in Southern Illinois spoiled a debate for him."

His next debate was near North Manchester, Ind., with William S. Manville, a minister of the Christian (Newlite) church. It began February 17, 1875, and lasted for nine days. In all, ten propositions were discussed, the most important of which was the following which Brother Robert affirmed: "Do the Scriptures teach the doctrine of the trinity, three persons or divine powers?" Intense interest was manifested in the long discussion. All reports show that the experience was pleasant. During the debate three persons were baptized by the Brethren.

In June of the same year he was called to Gogginsville, Va., to discuss the question of baptism by immersion with Daniel Hodges, a Methodist minister. The debate had its origin in a written discussion on this subject through the county paper, between Rev. Hodges and Elder John Lemon of the Church of the Brethren. The discussion became so warm that a public debate was sought, and Brother Robert was secured to defend our principles. The debate lasted three days and it is said to have been attended by a thousand people. In the afternoon of the last day a large crowd convened at the water to witness Brother Robert baptize a man known throughout the country as Jack Peters, who had been converted during the debate.

A local paper, the *Virginia Monitor,* characterized Brother Robert as follows: " The Rev. Mr. Miller is about 49 years old, of medium size and has a pleasant and intelligent appearance. He is a clear reasoner and evidently a practical debater." The late Dr. C. H. Balsbaugh gives his impression as follows: " In reading the speeches of these disputants I was frequently reminded of the famous debate between Lincoln and Douglas. On the one side, sobriety and confidence of truth; on the other, adroitness, evasions, circumlocutions and the ipse dixit of a sinking cause. The discussion cannot fail to bring into contempt with many ingenuous inquirers, the practice of sprinkling and pouring. Brother Miller's arguments are direct, consistent, conclusive."

In a private letter to Brother Robert, Dr. Balsbaugh reproved him somewhat for an expression that savored of boasting. The former replied to the charge in the following letter: " I admit your criticism to be correct, that without doing violence to the language referred to it may be construed into self laudation, though that was not the object, for I think there is nothing of that in my nature. It was the offshoot of my combative nature, the outcropping of that retaliative spirit of which I have a little too much to keep always in subjection when the provocation is so often repeated as was done by Mr. Hodges. During the discussion he frequently alluded to trine immersion in a sarcastic manner while it had no connection with the proposition; so I loosed the lion of combativeness to retaliate and it roared a little too loud. I should have used the spirit of the immaculate Lamb, for God's own Word is a sword more powerful for good than combative darts. But when Mr. Hodges made the State of Indiana, trine immersion, and myself a kind of racetrack on which to play when he was out of argument, my nature was not quite smooth enough to meet him without an effort to give him a spicy retort, and it was my feeling at the time to let it be known that I did not fear to meet the greatest man he could bring in a discussion on trine immersion. I admit it savors a little of boasting more than justifiable even under the circumstance; but it was not my greatness but the strength of the cause that dispelled my fears."

In February of the next year, he held a debate in Miami County, Ind., with Elder Aaron Walker of the Disciple church. Brother Robert believed that this was one of the strongest efforts ever put up against him; but he felt satisfied with the outcome. Elder Walker was an experienced debater, and had been present when Brother Robert held the debate with Elder Jewell. Brother Robert, knowing that Elder Walker would have able help, desired the presence of Elders James Quinter and J. H. Moore. In this he was disappointed, but when he arrived he found present Brother J. G. Royer, who then lived at Monticello, Ind. The latter served as Brother Robert's moderator and rendered him valuable assistance. This was the first they had ever met. Between the two there sprang up a fast friendship, which was terminated only when Brother Robert closed his eyes in death at the home of Bro. Royer, at Mt. Morris, Ill., sixteen years later.

Brother Royer's review of the debate was as follows:
" When the discussion opened, Elder Walker, with his able assistants, was early at the place, ready to enter upon the work with all confidence. Brother Miller, detained by missing connection, and being obliged to walk a half dozen miles over rough roads, came late; and when he did arrive was much fatigued. Both, however, entered upon their work with very good feelings and a zeal that was praiseworthy. They seemed to realize that they had a work to perform and threw their energies into it. And while they were engaged doing their best, they gave every student of human nature a favorable opportunity to contrast their widely different temperaments and compare the degree of Christian refinement in character as was exhibited during the discussion. Elder Walker, a man of ordinary height, and from what I saw and heard, of ordinary attainment, called into use his spacious lungs, his skill to press home arguments by explosive, vociferous and repeated gesticulation. Brother Miller, in his calm, earnest, inviting, yet pointed mode of delivery, framed and set up to full view his own arguments, and held up for criticism those of his opponent in such a way that forced the conviction home to the heart of every thinker that he was honestly seeking to defend the truth. This straightforward, unassuming, truth-crowned manner of meeting the issue and his unwillingness to compromise with error, won him many friends and we trust many more for the truth. When the final negative was closed, a very solemn feeling prevailed throughout the assembly and not a few tears stole their way over the cheeks of many present."

In all eight propositions were discussed based upon baptism, feet-washing, the Lord's supper and the holy kiss. Large crowds were in attendance and following the debate many were received into the church.

Eleven years later, October, 1887, these same debaters met in a five days' discussion in the Kilbuck church, Delaware County, Ind. Both the Brethren and the Disciples wanted the " Setting up of the kingdom " discussed. Elder Walker refused to accept the proposition, frankly admitting that he did not believe the doctrine of his own church on this question. He also told Brother Robert that he would never debate the subject of the holy kiss with him again. On the subjects of baptism, feet-washing and the Lord's supper, both earnestly contended for the truth as they saw it. It was during this discussion that Elder L. T. Holsinger, then a young man, received from Brother Robert that spirit and training for polemical discourse that later made him a worthy successor to the old veteran when the latter laid his armor by. Speaking of the debate, Bro. Holsinger says: " I recall very distinctly his calm discussion with Aaron Walker, and the Christian courtesy shown his opponent, and the clear, clean, though keenly-pointed arguments given. In addition to these qualities there was a very sacred and sanctified dignity in all his discussion, free from ridicule, which could not be said of his opponent."

In August, 1882, Brother Robert held a debate in Newton County, Mo., with Elder Morgan of the Disciple church. The latter positively refused to discuss the holy kiss and seems to have been considerably frustrated at various times during the week. However, in a report to his own church paper, he spoke of the debate as a pleasant experience and had only words of highest praise for his able opponent.

His last debate was held with Elder Daniel Sommer of the Disciple church, near Rockingham, Ray County, Mo., beginning March 20, 1889, and continuing eight days. Five propositions were discussed;

1. The Scriptures teach that the kingdom, or Church of Christ, was set up on the day of Pentecost, spoken of in the second chapter of the Acts of the Apostles. Daniel Sommer affirmed, R. H. Miller denied.

2. The Scriptures teach trine immersion as it is observed in the German Baptist or Brethren church.

3. The Scriptures teach feet-washing as an ancient custom or act of hospitality, or good works, to be observed as it is done in the church represented by Daniel Sommer.

4. The Scriptures teach that the salutation of the holy kiss is an ordinance to be observed as it is done by the German Baptist or Brethren church.

5. The Scriptures teach the bread and cup of the communion is the Lord's supper to be taken on the Lord's Day only, as it is observed in the church represented by Daniel Sommer.

This debate was published in book form which has had a wide circulation and is therefore more familiar to the public than his other debates, though several were published in the current periodicals at the time they were held. Elder Sommer was a man of bold appearance, rapid in speech, cutting in language. He evidently was not a man who depended upon strength and number of arguments to carry his point, but rather upon a great elaboration of some minor details. How the people passed their verdict on the debate can best be told by the fact that within two years there were nearly fifty accessions to the Church of the Brethren, while the church represented by Daniel Sommer had barely held its own.

In addition to these debates, Brother Robert had under consideration from time to time many other proposed debates that never came off. The Brethren in Missouri tried to get a debate between him and Elder D. B. Ray, a Baptist minister who later held a debate with J. W. Stein. It did not take place because Elder Ray would not accept clearly-defined propositions. At the time of his death Brother Robert had a debate under consideration as soon as his health would permit. His logical turn of mind caused him to demand propositions about which there could be no doubt as to the meaning. He always stayed to the proposition and demanded that his opponent do the same. He numbered his arguments and clearly defined them before bringing in the evidence. This gave his respondent a fair chance to answer every point. When a debate was proposed he always demanded that the denomination send forth its best man, and if possible a man of about his own age, so that there could be no plea, after the debate, that the other side did not have a fair chance. His other characteristics as a debater can be gleaned from accounts given above by those who were present to hear him.

Brother Robert's only written work, " The Doctrine of the Brethren Defended," gives in substance his main arguments in defense of the faith and practice of the church. The book was published in 1876, at a time when he was most active in his debates. In a letter addressed to the brethren through the *Primitive Christian* February 3, 1876, he states his purpose of the book:

" By permission I will say to the Brethren that I have a book which, as many of you know, has been in contemplation for some time. It contains the defense of our faith and practice, which I have tried to make in the discussions I have had. Having been frequently called upon by our brethren to engage in public discussions, some brethren may think I sought such controversy; but that is not the case. I have never got into it on my own account, as the brethren know, where such discussions have been held. I always advise to engage in discussion only when the church believes the cause will suffer without it, and then only as a matter of defense.

" The book we now offer to the Brethren is on the following topics: The Divinity of Christ and the Holy Spirit, Immersion and Affusion, Feet-washing, the Lord's Supper, the Holy Kiss, Nonconformity or Plainness of Dress and Secret Societies. These subjects are so investigated as to give the arguments on both sides, and show, when they are fairly examined, that the doctrine and practice of the Brethren are founded on Divine Truth."

This book was a silent worker wherever it went. It was a thorough, logical and masterly defense of all the peculiar doctrines of the Church of the Brethren. Many who were not yet in the church read the book and were fully convinced of its truth. It has done much to establish the doctrine of the church. It is an indispensable volume to the library of every minister of the Fraternity. It is and for years to come will likely be the standard work of defense for the church.

## CHAPTER III.

### Editorial Work.

The younger generation of the Church of the Brethren cannot remember a time when there was any recognized church paper other than the *Gospel Messenger*. But within the memory of our older brethren there have existed more than a dozen periodicals, at least eight of which were being published at one time. Throughout the first half of the nineteenth century no church paper was published. Of the definite history of the church during this period we know but little.

On April 1, 1851, the first number of a new paper called the *Monthly Gospel Visitor* was sent out from a press at Poland, Ohio. The editor and proprietor was Elder Henry Kurtz. For many years he had felt the need of such a publication; but as many of the brethren were suspicious of all innovations, the work was never brought forth until the above date. The Annual Meeting recognized the movement as a private undertaking and advised forbearance on the part of those who could not see the need of the paper.

The *Gospel Visitor* steadily grew in circulation and influence. Elder James Quinter became associate editor in 1856, and eight years later, when Elder Kurtz retired from active duties, Elder Quinter became acting editor. The paper continued its monthly visits until Jan. 1, 1874, when it was consolidated with another paper that had grown up in the meantime.

During the early years of the *Gospel Visitor* H. R. Holsinger was an assistant in the office. His observations caused him to feel the need of a weekly religious paper among the brethren. The proprietors, however, did not see fit to make the change and young Holsinger returned to Pennsylvania. He taught school in winter and worked on the farm in summer till 1863. Then after editing a secular newspaper for one year, he sent forth specimen copies of the *Christian Family Companion*. The policy of the paper was a broad one and much trouble arose because of the freedom with which discontented members were allowed to express themselves through its columns. This paper later became a regular weekly visitor and continued under the above name until June 1, 1874, when it was consolidated with the *Gospel Visitor*, the new publication retaining both of the names of the old papers.

The editors of the *Christian Family Companion and Gospel Visitor* were James Quinter and J. W. Beer, who stated on the title page that the paper was published by permission of "The Church of the Brethren." The paper was published at Dale City, later known as Myersdale, Pa. The name of the consolidated paper was soon found to be too long to be convenient and on Jan. 1, 1876, the name *Primitive Christian* was given to it.

In the meantime another paper had been making weekly visits since 1870. This was the *Pilgrim*, published by Brumbaugh Bros., at James Creek, Pa. On Oct. 24, 1876, this paper was merged into the *Primitive Christian,* which was now published at Huntingdon, Pa., by Quinter and Brumbaugh Bros. It continued under this management until June, 1883, when it was consolidated with the *Brethren at Work,* the new periodical being given the now familiar name of *Gospel Messenger.*

The *Brethren at Work* had its beginning in January, 1876, at Germantown, Pa., with J. T. Myers and L. A. Plate as editors of a small paper known as the *Brethren's Messenger.* In August of the same year it was moved to Lanark, Ill., and the name was changed to *Brethren at Work,* with J. H. Moore, J. T. Myers and M. M. Eshelman editors. Many changes were made in the editorial staff before the consolidation. Its course was conservative and it held much the same position in the West that the *Primitive Christian* held in the East.

Meanwhile other publications were begun with various purposes in view: the *Pious Youth,* the *Golden Dawn,* the *Young Disciple, Children at Work,* the *Youth's Advance* and *Our Sunday School* were papers published in the interest of the young people and the Sunday school. These periodicals either ceased to exist or were gradually consolidated until only the *Young Disciple* was left in 1883. The *Vindicator* was first published in March, 1870, for the purpose of battling against worldliness and all innovations. It has continued ever since, being at present the organ of the Old Order Brethren. The *Bruderbote* was a paper for the German brethren and sisters, and was at first issued in connection with the *Brethren's Messenger* and the *Brethren at Work.* Later it was moved to Grundy Center, Iowa, where it was published for fourteen years. The *Deacon* was a monthly published for two years at Lewisburg, Pa., with the purpose of working against the usurpation of authority on the part of aspiring elders. The *Brethren's Advocate* was a weekly of general church news, published for several years at Waynesboro, Pa., by D. H. Fahrney.

After the *Christian Family Companion* passed into the hands of Elder James Quinter, the "Progressive" element of the church had no organ through which they could express their views. To provide such a paper, Elders J. W. Beer and H. R. Holsinger began the *Progressive Christian* at Berlin, Pa., in 1878. Financial difficulties beset the proprietors and several changes were made in the management. In 1880 Elder Holsinger became sole editor and proprietor, and when the division of the church came, the *Progressive Christian* was moved to Ashland, Ohio, its name was changed to the *Brethren's Evangelist,* which is still the church paper of the Progressive Brethren.

The *Brethren's Evangelist* was the result of consolidating the *Progressive Christian* and the *Gospel Preacher*. The latter had been started in 1879, at Ashland, Ohio, and its proprietors were the trustees of Ashland College. There were many changes of editors who made the policy of the paper progressive or conservative as their own belief directed. When the division became evident and the majority of the trustees were in sympathy with the Progressives, both school and paper were won for that movement.

Considering the ability and prominence of Elder R. H. Miller, we should hardly expect him to be a silent reader during this period of change and prolific output of church papers. Neither was he inactive, though he is not remembered so much for his work in connection with the press as in other fields. Of the various publications already described, he was actively associated with three. In January, 1877, he became associate editor of the *Brethren at Work*. His writings were many during this year. The gist of several of his best sermons appeared in this paper. This was also the period of his active debating. His book, "The Doctrine of the Brethren Defended," had just appeared. Many attacks were being made on various regulations by members within the church. Consequently there was much demand for a strong defense of the principles of the church and the decisions of Annual Meeting. To make this defense, no brother was called upon as much as Elder R. H. Miller.

In the latter part of 1877 his work was changed from associate editor of the *Brethren at Work* to that of special contributor, which he continued to be for nearly two years. During a part of this time he was little heard from because of much sickness and death in his family. For the year 1880 he was editor of the western department of the *Primitive Christian*. These pages were rich in important church news, earnest defense of the principles of the church and much of his extensive correspondence.

January, 1881, found Brother Robert as one of the editors of the *Gospel Preacher* at Ashland, Ohio, the two senior editors being S. H. Bashor and J. H. Worst. The former ceased being a member of the editorial staff May 3, and on July 26 J. H. Worst bade adieu with the following explanation:

"It will be observed with this issue a change is

made in the editorial management of the *Preacher*, which may require an explanation. The trustees have decided to manage the college in harmony with the established usages of the church, so called conservative, and desire the paper to work in harmony with their decision. Since we do not feel willing to contend for all the established usages of the church, our policy being to say nothing either way upon some of the troublesome issues, it was thought best to unite the paper and school more closely. So the proposition was made to us to buy or sell. We sold, and Brother Miller will hereafter control the *Preacher*."

In the same issue Brother Robert outlined his plan for conducting his editorial work as follows: " In assuming the management of the *Preacher* as editor, we feel the responsibility to be so great that we need the councils and help of all who are working for the peace and prosperity of our church. It is hardly necessary for us to give our views upon the leading questions affecting its interests, as we have been working with the general Brotherhood for nearly a quarter of a century. In our annual councils, and in our papers we have freely given our views on all the leading questions. We have used whatever influence we have had to maintain the established order of the church, and the doctrines of the Gospel as understood by it. Our object will be in the future, as it has been in the past, to make our paper a means of maintaining our principles in that spirit and with that fraternal feeling which the highest interest of our church demands."

Faithfully did the editor attempt to carry out this policy. It was a period that tried an editor's soul.

Many correspondents desired to air to the general Brotherhood their own personal troubles and church difficulties. Over-enthusiastic brethren desired to rush into print articles that attacked the decisions of Annual Meeting. Many unkind words were said. Brother Robert was little disturbed by such as these. He endeavored to pour the oil of kindness upon the troubled sea, but nevertheless stood square at the helm and spoke with no uncertain sound in defense of the church. He was, however, much annoyed by the office clerk, who was Progressive in sympathy, and who frequently changed or omitted parts of the editor's work. On Nov. 29, 1881, David Baily and Edward Mason were announced as editors of the *Gospel Preacher* and the following explanation appeared from the former editor:

"We now retire from the business relation and editorship we have held in the *Gospel Preacher*. It is just to all that we give our reasons for so doing. When we went into the paper it was agreed by the owners and editors and made a part of the platform that it should be run in harmony with the councils and general usages of the church. In that way, as our people know, we have labored for the success of the paper and the cause of the Brotherhood. But the owners of the paper have lately concluded to run it more in the interest of the party calling themselves 'Progressives.' We cannot, neither are we under any obligations to work as editor, or give support to the paper when it changes from the platform which held it in harmony with the general Brotherhood. For nearly a quarter of a century we have worked in Annual Conference with our leading brethren such as Quinter, Eby, Saylor, Wise and many more like them, who have spent their lives working for the union and harmony of the church in the general councils. We cannot leave these faithful brethren and the principles they have so long labored with us to maintain.

"We came here to try to help our brethren direct the paper and the college in the interest of the church, and in harmony with its established usages; we have always avowed these sentiments and labored for them. None can say that we have changed or withheld our views, but we have ever openly and honestly contended for the union and harmony of our Brotherhood on the basis of the Gospel, to be applied and carried out by the general councils of the church. Though we lose our position as editor, we cannot in this day of their trial turn away in the least from Annual Conference, our leading brethren and the established usages they endorse. We believe the only true and gospel progression ever made in our church has been made by our leading brethren working with Annual Conference and the general Brotherhood. The Danish Mission, the Home Mission work, Sabbath-school work, and education have all been encouraged and supported by brethren who are loyal to the church and its established usages.

"We do not make personal warfare with those brethren owning the *Preacher,* but tell them we cannot give our support to any paper that does not work in harmony with the principles of the general Brotherhood. We shall continue to advocate the consolidation of all our papers that are loyal to Annual Conference

## EDITORIAL WORK 49

and the order of the church. In the meantime, I shall write occasionally in defense of our church and the principles it has held sacred since our connection with it. And if God will be our helper, we shall continue to work with these brethren and for the principles, and in harmony with the councils of our Brotherhood."

Soon after this Brother Robert resigned the presidency of Ashland College and made arrangements to move to North Manchester, Ind. In the meantime he accepted a position on the editorial staff of the *Brethren at Work* for 1882. His coeditors were M. M. Eshelman and Joseph Amick, with J. H. Moore, office editor. For a part of this year his pen was quite active but he did not care to renew the contract for 1883. Jan. 2, the following tribute to his work appeared:

"Brother R. H. Miller's time, for which he was employed as an editor, expired with the last issue. We part with regrets. We have always admired his ability as a writer and speaker, believing him to be among the ablest defenders of the Scriptures in the Brotherhood. He has our best wishes for the future and we hope to hear from him frequently, knowing that his writings on doctrinal questions and scriptural expositions are greatly appreciated in the Brotherhood."

After this he almost ceased to contribute for any of the papers, so much so that frequent queries were made as to why so able a man was silent. It was not that he was idle, for correspondent notes show that these were busy days for him among the churches. In July, 1885, he, together with S. S. Mohler and Daniel Hays, appeared on the advisory committee for the

*Gospel Messenger,* a position he continued to hold until his death.

Brother Robert always preferred talking to writing. Had it not been for this we would likely have much more important literature from his pen. His editorials did not cover a wide range of subjects. They were largely confined to questions that were prominent before the Brotherhood at that time. They were always on the side of the decisions of the church and no doubt wielded a great influence in those days of upheaval and change. Many of them possess as much value today as they did then. Some representative ones are included in this volume, with the hope that the reader will be edified with some of the best things said by him who once was eagerly listened to by thousands.

## CHAPTER IV.

### SELECTIONS FROM EDITORIALS.

#### DEFEND THE TRUTH WITH KINDNESS.

A sour, crusty look, a harsh, unkind word may destroy the greatest power for good we possess and leave the truth to suffer. To defend the truth with kind, pleasant words, with a meek, affable spirit, is of as much importance as to use argument. The truth always needs argument to sustain it, but no less does it need your kindness and affection manifested in all your words and actions.

#### SEEK FOR THE TRUTH.

The object for which men seek is of great importance, because they generally find or think they find the object for which they seek. If they seek for the simple, plain truth of the Gospel, for its commands and duties, they can easily find them. If they seek for some excuse or reason for not obeying it, they are likely to find the excuse. If they seek for some plan of salvation without obedience, they will likely find that plan. If they seek for non-essentials, they will soon find them. The infidel seeks for objections to the Bible, and he finds them. It is apparently strange how men find, or think they find, in the Bible almost any notion they seek for. They try to prove from it a hundred conflicting views, and seem to find the evidence they seek for. The only safe way to study the Book of God is in search for its truth, not to search it for evidence to prove a certain opinion, but with a determination that every opinion must bend to its truth.

### SYMPATHY.

Jesus is the example of sympathy as well as every other grace. His divine compassion filled his tender, feeling heart with sympathy for a suffering, dying world. This sacred compassion should tune our hearts with sympathy for those who slowly tread the path of sorrow or linger on its borders of suffering, or fall beneath its imperfections. Sympathy is a God-given and blessed power to help. When no earthly balm or gift can afford relief, sympathies can come with angel wings, and go beyond the reach of temporal help to comfort and sustain when all other power knows no relief.

How cold and icy and foreign from God is the heart devoid of sympathy. What a chilling breath it blows, sinking deeper those already in trouble. How poorly fitted is such a heart to reform the erring, with no sympathy for them in their imperfections and temptations. Sympathy costs but little, yet its worth cannot be measured in helping to lift the load of suffering, to lighten the burden and care that presses many a heart. Then let sympathy be cultivated and encouraged in its great mission of good, because its work is directed most where it is needed most.

## FORGIVENESS.

The duty to forgive, when it is asked and when it is due, is one of the most important duties in our experience. Jesus tells us if we will not forgive one another our Father in heaven will not forgive us. The heart that will not forgive others has no promise of forgiveness. One who fully realizes the joy in God's pardon of sin, and feels that all his own sins are atoned for by the blood of the Lamb, and pardoned in his mercy, feels that it is a blessing to forgive as well as to be forgiven. The noble, Christlike disposition to forgive with gladness of heart is the charity that suffereth long and is kind. Kindness that forgives after long suffering is richer because of the suffering, better because it has been tried and brings us nearer to Christ; because it is but another step in his example. The little partial forgiveness that we sometimes hear, "I'll forgive but I'll never forget," is not Christlike; it is a token of something smothered, to burst forth again and burn out all the forgiveness. It has none of the traits of pure forgiveness; neither the effects of forgiveness known and realized. Sin and forgiveness bring the sinner and the forgiver near together; and when it is pure, binds them closer together.

## SELF IMPROVEMENT.

Here is a large field and a subject of importance. That we all need improvement is as certain as that we are all imperfect. The first thing in the work of improving ourselves is to see our imperfections. To see our own faults is a blessing, because it is the first step toward getting rid of them. Many persons have faults they cannot see; in fact it is generally our misfortune that we are blind to our own imperfections. But this is true, mainly because our efforts in that direction are not very strong. We are too apt to see others' faults and neglect our own.

But self improvement does not consist alone in seeing our faults and condemning them; it must go farther to be a sure success. We must see and realize fully the opposite to our faults, the virtue and grace in that better quality which announces our faults. There is an opposite to every fault. That opposite is the right which we must learn to love and esteem so highly that its power becomes ever present to help give us the victory over our faults. Hence we need not think too much or dwell too long on our faults, but rather on their opposite. Let your mind dwell on all those noble qualities which overcome our faults.

This victory must be gained not merely by our own but by divine aid. To gain that, we need the throne of grace; and more, we need to have Christ with all the perfection of his life and love before us to lead us higher, till we rise above our own imperfections and live in a pure region of love ourselves.

Some people are very censorious, always finding faults in others and never looking after their own. They never do much except to try to pull down what others do. They see faults in all the work others are engaged in, but they never see their own faults or try to make themselves better by looking for some good they may do. These persons are likely to have one **great** fault at home, that of wanting to lead, and if they are not leading they will not work at all, except to pull down. They need humility of spirit to save them. Self improvement in this would help many a faultfinder to do much more good in the world.

WHOSOEVER CALLETH ON THE NAME OF THE LORD.

The importance of this text is often overlooked and misapplied. In it, calling on the name of the Lord is an expression which means calling upon the Lord. It teaches us to call upon the Lord in all that we do. Call upon the Lord to teach us what to do and how to do his will. Some people apply this text to the sinner, and have him converted, simply by calling upon the Lord. The application falls far short of the apostle's meaning. It is not only calling that God requires of us, but to hear and obey as well. This will lead us to the true meaning, that there is a right way to call upon the Lord, which we should apply to everything we do. Call upon the Lord to know if it is right to do this or that. Let the Lord decide for us.

This will insure our work to be right. Make it according to God's will and we shall be saved. Call upon him in all our doubts, in all our troubles, in all our objects and purposes. If a man should ask me to join a secret society I should call upon the Lord about it. If he says go into it, I would. If he did not make a secret society, I would not join one. If he did not go into one, I would not. I would call upon the Lord about it, hear him and do as he has done. Some one may tell me that I may be saved without baptism. I shall not dispute with him about it. I will call upon the Lord to see if he was baptized, and if he commanded others to be baptized. I would call upon him about it, not to give me a revelation, but to lead me to his Word and help me obey it.

### THE DANGERS PAST AND FUTURE.

In all the ages past, history shows that one great danger has ever beset and often destroyed the purity and holiness of God's people. That danger has been, and is in the one thing of running away from God's Word, and going over to the ways of the world. In this way Israel was led to worship idols. The world around the habitations of Israel walked in citadels, which often induced Israel to fall into the popular current and turn away from God.

After the gospel kingdom was set up it spread over a large portion of Europe and Asia Minor. But soon in the early ages of the church the signs of the early turning away from God to idolatry were seen repeating themselves when the church was merged into the world. In the days of Constantine the pure religion of Jesus was run into the political government, until the customs and civil governments of the world so overrun the church that its beauty and purity was left and its light gave out during the dark ages, because the church had gone over to the world in all its customs and purposes.

Our remedy to redeem the church and restore it back to its primitive purity and to God is reformation. Luther, one of the great reformers of modern times, found the church carried over into the world in its policies, its pride and fashion. He raised his voice against those departing from the Gospel, and organized a plain church which remained so for a long time.

John Wesley was a reformer in his day; he found that the Episcopal church had gone over to the world in all its ways and customs until it really made the popular current of politics and pride its own highway. Wesley pleaded for reform and organized a plain body of devoted men; and the Methodist church was for many years as plain a people as any to be found, even down to a period within the memory of many now living.

William Penn, another reformer, found the popular church conformed to the world in its spirit of war and pride and everything where custom would lead. He organized one of the plainest of churches. Alexander Mack, another reformer, found the popular church in war, in politics, in pride and in vanity. He organized a church, plain in all its principles of non-conformity. These modern reformers like those of ancient times, found the one great danger that had brought ruin into the church from the beginning was in men seeking popularity with the world, and the world carrying the church over into all its customs. Thus instead of converting the world to the church, the church was converted to the world. The one great danger from which the church has suffered most, and now is suffering, is that of conforming to the world. For this reason the apostle tells us not to be conformed to the world, which means not to let the world control us. If the world controls us it will soon have us conformed to the world. If it controls our affections and desires, we will soon practice its evils in the name of religion. The only way to stand firm against the dangers of sin is not to let the world control us in anything that will conform us to it.

### PRINCIPLES OF MISSIONARY WORK.

The gospel means of carrying on the work of salvation is God's plan of redemption put into the hands of the church. To use all these means in the spirit and zeal of the primitive church is the only way to insure prosperity. But to neglect these means, or to ignore any part of them, is the parent of weakness and failure. In the apostolic age they used all the means that would avail anything in the great purpose of salvation. We should note carefully all the means they used, because it is wrong to neglect or oppose any part of God's plan in his work. There are a great many ways and means in God's plan; preaching, singing, exhortation, prayer. These were sustained by other means—time, study, food, raiment, money; all were means needed, given, used. Just what the great cause needed is what the primitive saints gave to keep the God-given work moving onward and upward. Any kind of help that was wanted and any way it could be given to help on the work of Jesus and save sinners was embraced by them, because the principles deep in the heart made a fountain of love overflowing to run out in every channel opened for the waters of life to flow. They were not so over particular about just the kind of help, neither about just the way it should be given, but the principle creates a fount of love that must run out. Some ways may be better, some may be easier, some may be individual, some may be united in councils, but all the ways that carry the Gospel to dying sinners are good enough in their proper place, for all are in the Gospel. We can easily find a church in council sending Paul and Barnabas. In the primitive days they were not over particular about plans, about some favorite mode, or still more intent on finding some fault in all plans. They were not continually halting and caviling about plans, condemning all, and doing nothing, while at their very door could be heard the knell of dying sinners all around.

This faintly illustrates the principle God has given to help on the work of saving souls: The vessel is wrecked, its load of passengers cast into the ocean helpless; some dying, some freezing with cold, some suffering with hunger and affliction, and some wounded. The noble spirit of love and sympathy would set you to work with all the power and means you have, to help and save them. You would give your time, food, raiment, money or anything you can to save them. You would not stand there with suffering and death all around you and give nothing, do nothing, because some of the plans are not just as you prefer; you would not stand there making excuses for yourself, and finding fault with those who are doing all they can by the best means they know how. You would not stand there with your arms folded, faulting the kind of help, or the way it was given, whether by individuals or by a council, while your fellow-men are dying for want of the very means you can give. Much more important still is the fact that Christ sanctified and exemplified the principle of divine love, and its condition and relation and work to save dying sinners, and to reach the spiritual wants of thousands who are bound down by the shackles of sin, and led down to death by the power of Satan. If you would use all the means, power, work, and help to relieve the temporal suffering because of your sympathy, how much more reasonable and Godlike that deep down in your soul should burn the flames of gospel love, to save the suffering sinner from a second death.

God did not call and convert you alone that you might be saved, but that you might, in union with the church, do something to save others. He did not convert Paul alone for his own salvation, but that he might work for the salvation of others. God did not create you alone for your own enjoyment to breathe, to eat, to sleep, to live only for yourself; but to work for his glory and the good of others. He did not make the bee just to live and fly, but to make honey. No selfish purpose is in the mind of God. Man was to do something for the benefit of his race. He works and gives time and money for the social and political good of others; but how much more important, lasting and grand that heaven-born, God-given principle of the soul, to work for the spiritual good and salvation of others. This is the surperlative mission of wants, with a plan or without it; they are only questions of policy, to be adopted as the principle demands them. This great principle in the heart does not halt at every plan unless *I* is at the head of it or can rule it; it does not halt at every mite to be spent, or meeting to be held, or dollar to be given unless it *knows* the plan is the best and success is sure and all is perfect work; but " cast your bread upon the waters," leaving God to bless and gather it. " In the morning sow thy seed, in the evening withhold not thy hand," for you cannot tell which will prosper, whether this or that; but work on according to the principle within. God can use your feeble efforts, as he could use a raven to feed a saint, or a brazen serpent to save a sinner.

### SPHERE OF YOUNG WOMEN.

There are many young ladies who think they are filling the highest circles in society when they fill the ballroom, and display all the gewgaws of fashion. Adorning themselves in jewels and style, they make a fine display of etiquette abroad. A large circle in society they try to fill, and most of it away from home. They make more display in the party, the theater, and places of pleasure than they do of happiness and help at home. When such young ladies leave the burdens of home, with all its cares to rest on their mother, and they only fill the parlor, to play music and chat for company, or seek for similar pleasures in a wider circle, they never make home happy nor help bear its burdens. But at great cost their life goes on without usefulness or profit. When they marry, if they ever should, servants must wait on them still, and the parties go on or their happiness is done. If they never marry, by and by that fine circle will not want them, and they cannot come back to usefulness, and life becomes a burden because it is without any good or pleasure; all because she did not fill the true sphere of a young woman.

The proper sphere of the young woman is in the home circle and home work in life, in the family, the church and the school; her refining influence over her brothers, her help to supply their wants, care for their morals, refine their natures, and direct their lives, is a blessing to the family no other can supply.

Her work in the church is no less important. The young lady who is devoted to the cause of Christianity, regular to attend all the church services, its prayer meetings and Sabbath schools, wields an influence that no other can, and by her active labor does a work for society that spreads blessings all around her. The work of such a young woman, visiting the sick, showing kindness to the old and feeble, helping the poor, showing sympathy and giving comfort to the sorrowing, a servant in the kitchen or at the bedside of affliction, or wherever her kind hand can help or her kind words can comfort—such a young woman is worth a thousand butterflies of fashion, because she fills the proper sphere of a young woman. If she should marry, she is a blessing to her husband and in reality God's best gift to man. She is happy because the duties of life and usefulness in the world is the source of her happiness. She lives not for pleasure and show, but for the happiness derived from duty.

In the schoolroom is another circle the young lady may fill and adorn with all her graces, to bless those around her; and if she never marry this is probably the most useful field of her labors. She may continue all her good work in the church, and in the world around her home, living a life of happiness in the pathway of duty and usefulness.

### CHURCH DEDICATION.

I have just returned from Cerro Goro, Ill., where I went on Dec. 1 [1878] to dedicate the new church.

Brother John Metzger built it with his own means except a part of the basement and a little work. This is a noble example of liberality and love for the church. Some of you readers will wonder how a church is dedicated. Well, I cannot tell what others say or do, but I can tell them how we did it. One of the brethren opened the meeting as is common with us and then I tried to preach on the following:

1. God has built a church on earth embracing all the truth and righteousness there is for man's sanctification and happiness. To that church the Christian should look in all his work for the good of man. In the cause of temperance the Christian should carry his work into the church; in his charities, go to the church; in his life's work, take all into the church; turn it over to God, and by his authority govern all your life. You need no other organization or secret society to divide your time, strength, talent, means, thus robbing God of his rightful service.

2. How should the Christian conduct himself in the Lord's house? It is a place for worship, not to meet for conversation on worldly matters, to talk of farming, etc., but a solemn, sacred place for singing praise and worshipping in spirit and in truth. You should feel the house of God so sacred that as soon as you enter the door, you take off your hat in honor to Christ, your Head, for thus you should pray or prophesy, says the apostle.

3. The house should not be desecrated by worldly amusements. Never allow church festivals, Christmas trees, and like amusements to be held there to gratify the vanities of fashion. Let everything that is

said or done in this house be to the glory of God. This church was built for the brethren where the plain teaching of God's Word is to be carried out in its primitive purity.

4. This is a plain church; and in it we hope a plain people will always meet to worship. Plainness of dress, as taught in God's Word, will make this church a suitable place for rich and poor to meet in one common brotherhood, where pride, fashion, or wealth do not destroy the peace and prosperity of God's people.

5. Let this church be the home of your affections, around this altar with God's children come and bow in prayer; come and sing; come and hear the Word of Life. Come with your influence and counsel to help build up the cause and save souls.

About in this way we preached, then closed by prayer, thanking God for the pleasant place we had to worship, and asking him to help the brethren keep the church pure and holy; that the primitive faith and practice of the Gospel may ever be the established order of the church, that the Holy Ghost may reign in their hearts, rule over their lives, and be their Comforter when the powers of earth have failed.

So this meeting ended, and they call it dedicating a church. I do not know that there will be any fault found unless it will be in the word dedication and before this is done we hope the subject will be looked at from a scriptural standpoint.

### THE PLAN OF SALVATION.

Some articles written by Brethren Mohler, Myers and Moomaw, on doctrinal questions, have attracted

# SELECTIONS FROM EDITORIALS

special attention. And when there are different positions taken on the same question in a public journal, they cannot all be correct, and may be misleading in reference to the doctrine of the church; hence propositions should be carefully taken and clearly stated.

The special subject under investigation is the obedience of Christ to the will of God, the Father; whether there is any merit in his obedience to his Father's will in his observing and setting up the ordinances and duties of the church. No doubt is expressed by any regarding the merit of his suffering and death. The only difference seems to be in regard to the merit of his righteous and perfect obedience to his Father's will, during his life on earth. John 6:38. " I came down from heaven, not to do mine own will, but the will of him that sent me." His mission to our world was to do the will of the Father, and that will embraced all his life's work and his death.

The merit of Christ's righteous obedience, the question at issue, is an important one because of its bearing upon our own obedience to God's will. As this word merit does not occur in the Scriptures, we should be the more careful in its use and clear in the meaning we attach to it. I conceive it to be like this: A king offers to give a title to an estate if a man will build a house upon it according to the will of the king, who has specified every part of the building minutely as to its material and parts. Now if the man builds the house perfectly, according to the will of the king as specified, he has merited and has a right to the title promised by the king. Who could say there was not merit in every part of the work? The grade is 100 per cent. But suppose the man had failed in every specification of the master's will; the grade would not be 50 per cent. Now this man would have no right to claim the inheritance or any part of it. This is man's failure to render perfect obedience to the expressed will of God in every particular. There is no merit in poor man.

But Christ built the spiritual house perfect in every part and this has merited that eternal inheritance for us. "But Christ as a son over his own house; whose house are we, if we hold fast the confidence and the rejoicing of the hope firm unto the end." Hebrews 3:6. Thus Christ rendered perfect obedience to the Father's will, and in his righteousness as well as his death he merited the eternal inheritance, the spiritual house, and now offers to make us heirs with him on conditions, not on one condition. The perfect happiness of the redeemed is not merited by their own imperfect obedience, but by the perfect obedience of Christ. We believe this is the doctrine of the Scriptures and of the church.

There is a doctrine which we wish to notice. It puts all the merit in the death of Christ, applies that merit by faith, making the death of Christ and its application on condition of faith, the two essentials of salvation. This doctrine does not reject obedience, but holds obedience as non-essential on the human side, and of no merit on the divine side. We hold that all things done by the Father, Son and the Holy Spirit in giving the plan of salvation to man, have merit, power, blessing, and salvation in them because of their perfection. Hence we can in truth say with Paul, "The law of the spirit of life in Christ Jesus hath made me free from the law of sin and death." The law of the Spirit must have power and merit in it when it can make man free from the law of sin.

If then the merit of Christ consists in his obeying the will of the Father perfectly, that will becomes the higher law for Christ and for man. Paul gives the will of God a high position in Ephesians 1:11: "In whom also we have obtained an inheritance, being predestinated according to the purpose of him who worketh all things after the counsel of his own will." The precept and example of Christ in setting up the ordinances of the church is a part of the all things that are worked after the counsel of God's will. That will is absolute. It is by that will we are sanctified, though it is through the blood of Christ, through the work of the Holy Spirit, and through other means and conditions, yet it is all after the counsel of his own will.

The will of God as revealed by the Son and by the Holy Spirit is contained in his Word, giving the teaching and example of Christ and the inspired apostles. If the will of God were a matter of so much indifference till there was no merit in Christ obeying it, or if the will of God is not to be obeyed by us as conditions of our salvation, then the death of Christ might be sufficient or it might be applied by faith alone. But if it was necessary for Christ to obey the will of God to merit the salvation, and necessary that man come to the will of God and obey it as means of grace and condition of salvation, then must righteousness and obedience be set forth and manifested in the life of the Christian as it was manifested in the righteous and holy life of Jesus Christ.

### ANOINTING THE SICK.

This subject has been before the Brotherhood so much lately that we feel confident some are tired of it. And there has been no definite conclusion arrived at among the brethren to indicate a satisfactory settlement of the disputed question; so there is danger that some things will be advocated so strongly that they will not be edifying to the church or beneficial to the cause of truth. We ought to settle all the questions arising in reference to this subject on plain gospel principles, and we wish to look at the plain gospel teaching.

In all the commands of the Gospel there is a purpose of blessing. It is the duty of God's people to obey the command as it is taught in the Gospel; it is the work of God to give the blessing. The Bible is made up largely of duties and blessings, commands and promises, obedience and happiness. The work of man is on the side of the duties and commands; the work of God is on the other. To illustrate this truth, God will not believe for man; he must believe for himself and God gives the blessing. Man must repent and be baptized; God pardons his sin. So it is with all other commands and duties necessary to man's salvation.

Anointing the sick is like all other commands given with a design or object which God grants by his divine power. All these commands are means and conditions which God has appointed to accomplish certain ends. God has appointed faith, repentance, and baptism for the pardon of sin and the adoption into his kingdom.

The pardon of sin requires as much divine power as any miracle in the Gospel. But where there is a law of pardon, in which means and conditions are given to secure that end, shall we call that pardon a miracle? Or in any case where God gives a law and appoints the means and conditions upon which the divine blessing is promised, should we call the divine blessing a miracle? We say not, because it is given under a general law and applies to all who obey and the divine blessing is obtained through the means of grace appointed in the Gospel.

To illustrate: God has appointed the means by which we obtain his temporal blessing; to plant and sow and reap are but the use of means God has apappointed by and through which he will bless man in temporal things. Every good and perfect gift comes from God; and shall we call them all miracles, both temporal and spiritual? We say No. Where there is a command and a promise belonging to general law, it is a means of grace and not of miracles. All the commands and duties of the Gospel are means of grace. The apostle says, " Let us have grace." We obtain it by using the means given.

Although God gives his grace by divine power, we do not want the gift of grace called a miracle. We apply this faith and these principles when we anoint the sick. We use the means God has appointed, the anointing and the prayer, trusting God to bless by divine power the means he has appointed for the pardon of sin and the restoration of the body, I no more think of a miracle when I anoint a brother than when I baptize him. " The prayer of faith shall save the sick."

What is a prayer of faith? It is not that prayer that dictates to God what he shall do and how he shall do it, but that prayer that comes in obedience to the means, just as God has given them, and asks him to save and raise up the sick in his own way. Paul prayed three times for the thorn in the flesh to be removed; but God answered his prayer by giving him grace to bear it, which was much better. The prayer of faith gives God the whole case, to bless and save and raise up in the time and way his infinite wisdom appoints.

The working of miracles is a special gift direct from God. "To one the gift of miracles, to another the gift of healing, to another the gift of tongues." These are special gifts from God; but he has not appointed any means or commands in the Gospel on which he promises to give us these. If God had appointed the means to obtain these gifts like he has to obtain the pardon of sin, then we could all use the means and procure these gifts. But God has not given any means in the Gospel to procure these gifts, hence no man has them in our day. Take the gift of tongues; by no means can a man speak in a language he has never learned. It is just as plain but a little more difficult to see into the work of healing. If an elder should come to anoint the sick and say that the gift of healing was in himself or in his own faith and power, I should think of him about like I would if he should come to baptize, saying that the gift of pardon was in his own faith or prayer. We must look to the other side to see if the one who receives the ordinance is right in the sight of God. He receives all the blessing in baptism because they are gifts from God to him.

Though the administrator be an adulterer or a hypocrite, the man who receives it is blessed because he is right in faith. So it is in the anointing. The blessing does not depend on any virtue in the elders. They might be unholy men or void of common honesty without any shadow of the healing gift, but when the sick is right in the sight of God, his blessing is sure because he receives it through the means God has commanded.

The gift of miracles is a special power conferred upon one who officiates or administers in the power he possesses. All the effects of healing or any other supernatural work depends upon the power vested in the administrator. Not so in the ordinances of the Gospel. The pardon of sin and the healing of the body are in the anointing and do not depend upon the gift of healing in the elders. The healing is not the result of any power in the elders any more than the pardon of sin is the result of power in them. All the blessing comes from God through the means of grace he has appointed and there is no miracle about it though it is all of divine power. The sick saint calls for the elders and from them receives the ordinance as James commanded it. His sins are pardoned and he is restored to health.

The question might arise, Which was done first? Was he first pardoned and then healed or was he healed first, or did he receive both at once? Many other questions of similar import might be asked, but a discussion of them cannot be profitable. The great truth lies in a full obedience to the commands of God just as he has given them without any change by addition or subtraction. A full trust in God for his blessings is the strongest and surest foundation on which he can rest for time and eternity.

### THE PRAYER COVERING.

We here propose to examine what the apostle says in reference to the covering. He says, "But I would have you know that the head of every man is Christ; and the head of the woman is the man; and the head of Christ is God." Here are sacred relations which the apostle would have us know and observe so they may be manifest in our worship. Out of these sacred relations grow many important duties. The apostle speaks first of the relation between the man and the woman and continues that subject to the close of the sixteenth verse. He then takes up the relation expressed in the truth that the "head of every man is Christ," which he continues to the end of the chapter, all the time speaking of the ordinances as duties growing out of these relations. And the ordinances stand in the church to manifest the doctrine in these sacred relations; and when we obey from the heart the form of doctrine, we observe ordinances which represent the doctrine out of which the form grows. Hence the design of the ordinance is to represent or manifest a doctrine or truth which dwells in the heart.

One doctrine or truth the apostle " would have you know " is that " the head of the woman is the man." To manifest this relation the apostle teaches a covering to be worn by the woman in time of worship. The doctrine is that the man is the head of the woman and the relation or headship is shown by the covering. To avoid an error into which some have fallen, we observe that it is a relation between man and woman, and not the relation of a husband and wife that the apostle is speaking of. He does not mention "husband and wife" once in the chapter; but in the eleventh verse he refers to the man and woman "in the Lord," making no difference whether married or not married.

In the fourth verse Paul says, "Every man praying or prophesying with his head covered, dishonoreth his head." That is, he dishonors Christ by coming before him in worship with his head covered. This doctrine may be illustrated by the social custom of our own times. See those who come in the presence of the Governor, or President, take off their hats to honor him. See the man who comes into court or any assembly he thinks honorable take off his hat to show his regard. So the Christian man should feel that in the assembly of God's people, even more than earthly or social honors are due from him to Christ, his Head in the church, and uncover his head to manifest the doctrine in the heart. But we sometimes see this doctrine and its manifestations set aside by the custom of Christian men at funerals covering their heads, thus making void the commandment of God by the traditions of men.

In the fifth verse the apostle tells us how the covering shall manifest the doctrine that the man is the head of the woman in the Lord. "But every woman that prayeth or prophesieth with her head uncovered, dishonoreth her head." That is she dishonoreth the man because he is the head of the woman. To enforce the importance of this covering the apostle in the seventh verse brings up these relations in a different form: "For a man indeed ought not to cover his head forasmuch as he is the image and glory of God; but the woman is the glory of the man." This scripture alludes to the relations in the third verse, but instead of pointing to the head as chief object in the relation, it refers to the second object and points to the man who was created for "the glory of God," and to the woman who is created a new creature, as "the glory of the man." Man, then, is to manifest the glory of God by uncovering his head; and woman is to manifest the glory of God in the church by the covering on her head.

This covering to be worn by the woman in worship is on account of and grows out of her relation to man in the church. This relation is further brought to view in the ninth verse when he says, " Neither was the man created for the woman; but the woman for the man." Here we learn that the woman was created for the man and out of this relation there come many duties both in providence and redemption. For this relation spiritually we wish to look into God's Word. Woman was made a "helpmeet" for man. This means that man is the principal and that woman is his help. The term " meet " means equal and even. Though man is the head of the woman, she is the glory of the man when she is his help and his equal with the exception of the difference and limits made in divine law.

Under the Jewish dispensation all the blessings, spiritual and temporal, were given to the woman as well as to the man; but these blessings were given to the woman through a law whose ceremonies were administered by the hands of the man for the blessings and benefits of the woman as well as the man. The man was made priest to kill and offer the sacrifices. The ordinances of the Jewish law were administered by the man, not the woman; but the woman was made equal in the blessings and his help in the service. Still more is this sacred relation manifest in the gospel dispensation. The messiahship, the apostleship, the official work in the Christian church were all given to man, though all the blessings both spiritual and temporal reach the woman as well as the man. To administer baptism, to officiate at the communion, to ordain elders by laying on of hands, each is an official work given to man; yet he needs the help of woman, heart and hand, in all of his work.

The woman, man's helpmeet, should administer, observe and obey all the commands and duties which do not require a chosen official of the church to administer them. The Gospel also enjoins a number of duties and commands upon the woman that she may be a helpmeet to man. In the government of the church, the woman has a vote equal with the man, though to administer this government the man is made the head as well as in the administration of the ordinances. Our text shows that it is her duty to pray and to prophesy. In fact she is man's helpmeet in every gospel work limited only by that which explicitly requires an official of the church.

We want to illustrate the meaning of the headship of our text by civil government where every citizen is a voter and in a sense a sovereign; yet the officers who administer the government are the heads of their departments. One is at the head of the war department, another of the state department and so on. The government is administered by the heads of these departments. When our text says that the man is the head of the woman " in the Lord," it is the same idea applied to spiritual government.

There is another duty growing out of this relation when Paul says that the woman " was created for the man." It shows that the man is to provide for and take care of the woman. " He that provides not for those of his own house has denied the faith "; thus showing that the man must take care of the woman, not the woman take care of the man. And Paul tells Timothy that the widows must be taken into the highest favors of the church. These duties, resting on those who administer the government of the church, in taking care of the women, are taught in the Gospel the same as the husband's duty to take care of his wife. On this ground we may say that the husband is the head of the wife in the family; and so the man is the head of the woman in the Lord.

In the tenth verse Paul says, " For this cause ought the woman to have power on her head because of the angels." " For this cause " evidently refers to what he has said in the preceding verse, that the woman was created for the man. This word power is a translation of " exousian," which Greenfield says signifies an emblem of power, honor and dignity in this place. The expression occurs about one hundred times in the New Testament; about sixty times it is rendered power; about thirty times it is rendered authority; and in the other cases by jurisdiction, liberty, right and strength.

This shows clearly that it refers to that kind of power that refers to authority or jurisdiction. Benson, Macknight and Sharp as well as Greenfield understand it to mean an emblem, a token, or a mark to represent power, authority or dignity and shown by a veil, diadem or turban. This covering, on the head of the woman, is the sign of the power and authority over her in the church. It is the power to which she looks for the administration of its government, for her protection and blessing. This is the token of the power over her in God's spiritual kingdom; it is a sign and token of power in the man to administer the ordinances and government of the church. It is a sign of her submission and her faith and trust in God's plan of salvation for her.

This covering is made important because it is connected with the worship of God and is to be worn "because of the angels." These two reasons are enough to establish it as an order in the church and place it among the ordinances spoken of by the apostle in the beginning of the chapter. The nature and object of the covering is such that we cannot treat it with indifference and set it aside without showing disregard and disobedience to the Word of God.

We will now look carefully for a covering that will be a sign or emblem of the spiritual, divine and sacred power associated with the worship of the woman. Some persons talk and act as though anything would do for a covering; but this shows that they have not investigated the subject carefully. Would we dare say that anything would do as a sign or token of the power represented by the flag of the United States?

Certainly we would not, for nothing will do but the flag of freedom that waves by the authority of the power it represents. We dare not say that anything will do for the uniform of the soldier; because that uniform is a sign or token of the power that is over him when he is in the service. If the soldier throws away the uniform when he is in the service, he dishonors the power over him, or in the language of our text, he "dishonors his head."

Again, we cannot have a sign or token or emblem of anything without having an established order. If every Mason would wear just such sign as his taste would choose, you would have no sign of Masonry that anyone could recognize. If every soldier and officer in the army should choose according to his own preference something as a uniform or emblem of his office, you would have no uniform or emblem or sign that anyone would recognize. When you destroy an established order you cannot have a sign or emblem of anything.

Now why not admit the Word of God on the same principle of reasoning and acknowledge the law of God just as important and binding in reference to a sign or emblem as we do with reference to a worldly institution? The law of God on all subjects teaches by the letter and by the Spirit as well as by the example of inspired men. All these are to be combined and consulted in the investigation of every subject. Some seem willing to take the letter only as making law for their government. Others take the Spirit as they conceive it teaches and think the letter a matter of form that is of minor importance and may be changed or set aside without doing any wrong. These two extremes are likely to accept the example of inspired men only so far as it agrees with their views. But the whole truth requires that we take all the light God has given us by the letter, the Spirit and the example of inspired men.

The truth is certainly clear that the Spirit is the power from which the letter or word has come; and also the power which has given us the example of inspired men. All the commandments and duties taught in the Gospel are manifestations of the Spirit. The lives and example of inspired men are the manifestation of the Spirit that is in them. Just so the life and mission of Christ is the manifestation of the Spirit that was in him. And when we come to this sign or emblem in the covering for the woman, it is to manifest or show the Spirit, its doctrine and truth in the obedience of the woman.

The question now is, What shall the covering be? What will most perfectly and surely be a sign or token of the power to which the woman is subject in the Lord? It must be something that will represent the word and spirit of the Gospel. We have said before and we repeat it that a plain white covering is the only kind that surely and fully manifests the letter and spirit of revelation. That is must be plain, few devoted Christians will deny if they have carefully thought on the subject. The Gospel condemns all superfluity of gold, pearls and costly array. It must be a plain covering. But that it must be a white covering is doubted by some.

The most perfect condition of righteousness is represented by a similitude that is perfectly white. Isa. 1:13. "Though your sins be as scarlet, they shall be white as snow; though they be red like crimson, they shall be as wool." Here is scarlet and red representing sin, while the whiteness of snow and wool represents them as washed in the blood of the Lamb. In the 51st Psalm, David says, "Wash me and I shall be whiter than snow." Similar ideas are expressed in Dan. 12:10, Matt. 17:2, and in Rev. 7:14, 19:14, 18, etc. All these scriptures not only show that the saved condition of the Christian is represented by comparison to the purest white, but also the appearance of the Son of God, of angels and saints, manifests the righteousness within them by white raiment. It may also be observed that the appearance of Christ when he takes vengeance upon the wicked is as if clothed in a vesture dipped in blood. The blood manifests his judgment upon the wicked; while his white raiment manifests his salvation of the righteous.

Again in Rev. 17:4: "And the woman was arrayed in purple and scarlet color, and decked with gold and precious stones and pearls, having a golden cup in her hands full of abominations and filthiness of her fornications." Here is a woman which is a full manifestation of the wicked spirit in her. It is in direct contrast to the white emblems that represent the righteousness of the saints. We cannot conclude, therefore, that it would be consistent with the spirit of the Gospel to take the very ornament of this woman: the purple and scarlet, the gold and the pearls, or any part of it to be a suitable covering for the Christian woman when she comes before God in worship.

### CHURCH GOVERNMENT.

In the *Primitive Christian,* 1880, Brother Robert wrote a series of articles on church government. The articles are too long to insert in this work, but the heads of the different divisions of the subject are here given in his own words:

First. According to the Scriptures the church is an association of districts or congregations in one body. Hence it is an associate government and not congregational.

Second. The church in its government is republican in form and spirit. All its members, male and female, have a voice and vote in its councils and decisions. The smallest districts have a representation in its general councils, while they have entire control of all matters that are simply local.

Third. The church government is judicial and executive, not legislative. It decides upon matters brought before councils, according to the Gospel.

Fourth. In the government of the church there are five tribunals or councils in which a case or person may be tried; 1, in the local church; 2, in the local church with the adjoining elders; 3, the district meeting may appoint a committee; 4, the Annual Meeting may appoint a committee: 5, where a local church rejects a decision made by Annual Meeting committee, the case is appealed direct to the Annual Meeting. A case in which the humblest individual is involved may be appealed to the highest tribunal just the same as the highest officer in the church.

Fifth. The local church elects its own officers, ministers and deacons, who are installed into their office by the bishops. The local church also elects its delegates to the district and the Annual Conference. At all these elections both the brethren and the sisters vote. Those who are sent as delegates may be lay members of the church as well as officers. These officers of the church are the servants of the church, not the rulers.

Sixth. All the members have the right to express their mind, to give their views on all subjects brought before the councils of the church, either local or general. These rights granted to all the members of the church bring each of them under obligation to obey the decisions and councils of the church both local and general.

Seventh. This republican form of church government, making each member a councilor in all the business of the church, also makes it the duty of every member to work with and for the church in all its efforts for the conversion of sinners, the spread of the Gospel and for the maintenance of the decisions, rules and order that have been established in its councils, both local and general.

Eighth. This form or system of church government will bring to the people of God the greatest happiness possible for them in this life. They have one law given, one law and the council of one church to help them to follow that law with one mind and one judgment, and all speaking the same thing, making the church a power in the hands of God for good in the world, making each member a living epistle to be read and known by all men and a help to increase the happiness and peace and prosperity of the church.

## CHAPTER V.

### EDUCATIONAL WORK.

It is a matter of history that secondary and higher education did not meet with favor in the Church of the Brethren during the first half of the nineteenth century. The brethren, during the eighteenth century, were the equals of any of their neighbors in educational interests. The misfortunes of the church leaders during the Revolution and the liberal religious spirit of the times are the probable reasons for the brethren becoming antagonistic toward educational work. The question as to the propriety of brethren educating their children in a college was before the Annual Meeting in 1831 and was discouraged. In 1832, 1853 and 1857, similar queries pertaining to attending, establishing or teaching in high schools were answered also by disapprovals.

The sentiment for a higher education than that of the common school became too great to be resisted. A number of the leading brethren had had long experience in teaching school and saw the advantages of more advanced training. Among these brethren were Elder Henry Kurtz and James Quinter, editor and assistant of the *Gospel Visitor*. In 1857 these brethren moved the *Gospel Visitor* from Portland, Ohio, to Columbiana, in the same State. At the latter place they contemplated starting a school. At the Annual Meeting in 1858 the following query with its answer was passed:

"We desire to know whether the Lord has commanded us to have a school besides our common schools, such as the one contemplated in the *Gospel Visitor?* If we are, ought we not to have it soon? And if it is not commanded of the Lord, ought we to have one? And is it right to contend for or against such an institution publicly through the press, since our different views may become a stumbling block before the world? And if it is once decided ought we not to keep forever silent about it? Ans.—Concerning the school proposed in the *Gospel Visitor,* we think we have no right to interfere with an individual enterprise so long as there is no departure from gospel principles."

Brethren Kurtz and Quinter later decided that Columbiana was not a desirable location for a school and looked about for a better location. This was thought to be found at New Vienna, Ohio, where a brick building, that had been erected for an academy, was purchased by the brethren. Here Brother Quinter with several assistants opened a school Oct. 14, 1861. The school continued for nearly three years when it was closed on account of conditions resulting from the Civil War.

In the spring of 1861 Brother S. Z. Sharp had opened a school twelve miles southeast of Huntingdon, Pa., known as the Kishaquillas Seminary, which had been erected by the Presbyterians. At the end of seven years, Brother Sharp sold the seminary and went to Tennessee, where he remained ten years engaged in pastoral work and as a teacher in Maryville College. In 1870 Bro. O. W. Miller, who had been

## EDUCATIONAL WORK

Bro. Quinter's chief assistant at New Vienna, opened a school at Bourbon, Ind., known as Salem College. This school was the occasion of two queries coming before the Annual Meeting of 1871. The answers to the queries show the attitude of the church toward the colleges at that time.

"In 1871 Art. 3.—Does the Annual Meeting of 1871 claim Salem College of Bourbon, Ind., to be under the auspices of our Brotherhood? Ans.—It does not regard it as a church school, or conducted by the general Brotherhood, though it is under the auspices of members of the church and is supported by those who patronize it, and not by donations of the church."

"In 1871, Art. 27.—Is it advisable for a brother to serve as manager or teacher of a high school, as the tending thereof is to lead many of the brethren from the simplicity that is in Christ and also to divide the Brotherhood? Ans.—Inasmuch as the Annual Meeting has admitted the propriety of a high school, as a private enterprise, we cannot prohibit a brother from teaching in such an institution; and as regards the fears that many entertain of the tendency of such an institution to lead brethren from the simplicity of the church, this will depend upon the character of the institution. And to guard the Salem College against any such tendency, this Annual Meeting advises the elders of the church district in which the college is located to take into its charge all the teachers and scholars of said college who are members of the church, and require of them to conform to the general order of the Brotherhood."

Salem College continued for some time, and then

from a lack of funds, the property relapsed to its former owners. The next successful effort to establish a secondary school was made by Brethren Lewis Kimmel and Howard Miller at Plum Creek, Pa., in 1874. It continued four years and was then abandoned. In 1876 Brother J. M. Zook began a private school at Huntingdon, Pa. This was the humble beginning of what was to develop into the far-famed Juniata College. On the death of Brother Zook, in 1879, Elder James Quinter became president of the college.

When Plum Creek school came into financial need, Bro. Asa Packer of Northeastern Ohio, became interested in working for an endowment for the school. He visited Pennsylvania, but after some time returned to Ohio and began to interest brethren in the project of starting a school at Louisville, Ohio. Later Ashland, Ohio, a beautiful city of four thousand inhabitants, and surrounded by strong congregations of brethren, was selected as the best place for the new college. In the *Brethren at Work,* September 3, 1877, the following is a part of an announcment that was given: "Feeling the need of an institution of learning, affording sound, practical education, and at the same time free from the vanities and extravagance of boarding schools, many friends of education in the German Baptist Church intend to establish such a school at Ashland, Ohio."

The school opened in 1878 with Brother S. Z. Sharp president. After two years of successful work, Brother Sharp ceased to be president because of some differences between him and the trustees. The question of electing his successor was a difficult one. It was at the time when the progressive element was becoming active and brethren were suspicious of nearly all who were interested in higher education. Could a suitable man be selected for the head of the college, who at the same time could inspire confidence in the Brotherhood at large? The field was canvassed and the man whom the trustees finally selected was Elder Robert H. Miller.

The question for Brother Robert to decide now was whether he should accept. If he did, he would lose his influence with hundreds of the Old Order Brethren who were opposed to all higher learning. On the other hand he would likely come into conflict with those of the more progressive type, for which Ashland and Northeastern Ohio seemed to be the headquarters. Besides this the college was in serious financial trouble and the outcome was uncertain. Many of his friends advised him not to accept, and when he finally decided to do so it came as a surprise to many. His own explanation in the *Primitive Christian,* July 20, 1880, gives us his reasons for his decision:

"We have accepted a position in Ashland College as its president because we feel it our duty to do so under the circumstances. We have some institutions among us that will be a power for good if their influence is directed for the interest of the church. To oppose education in this age or to oppose these higher institutions of learning, is a vain effort that will injure the church by drawing many of her sons and daughters to other schools, where the principles of other denominations and the vanities of the world lead them away from the simple doctrines of the Gospel. We accept this position to help turn all the influence of education among us in favor of the simple and plain truths of the Gospel as taught by our Savior and as maintained by our church.

"We feel that all the means in our reach should be used to advance the cause of Christ. And there is nothing so great in importance as the proper training of the young; if that is lost all is lost. And we feel that our brethren whose heart is in the work fully, should help us in turning these institutions of learning to the mental, moral and spiritual welfare of the young, and to the advancement of the church. To oppose education in this age and this country is to die; though it may be slow it will be sure, because the rage of learning is all around us now; a free school for eight months in the year in reach of all, and higher schools all over the land. We must turn this training of the young to the truths and principles of Christianity. It must be done by us or be left undone till we see many of our brightest sons and daughters carried away with the world through the channels of education where the truths of the Gospel are not regarded. We want every science and art, and business and calling, all turned to help in the great work of saving men. We cannot do this by opposing them; we must take hold of them ourselves, rid out the evil, turn all the good to service for God. To this end we can do more in the proper training of the young than in any other."

A more simple, concise or a more thorough statement of what should be the attitude of the church toward the schools was never uttered. And today, after thirty years have passed, this position is more and more being realized. Elder I. D. Parker, who was one of the trustees of Ashland College while Brother Robert was president, characterizes his work for the college as follows:

"Having assumed the obligations, he calmly went forward and was a strong defender of the college interests when the trials came. Of these there were many and such as fully test men's souls. When others were excited and warmed up beyond control, he was always calm and cool. Others might use harsh and rough words, but he always met these with kind words and hard arguments. Not having a finished education, he knew well where he was lacking and was frank to admit it. This gave him the respect and confidence of all about him. He was very practical and resourceful on all occasions. His plans were well matured and were presented clearly and forcibly. When old or young went to him for counsel on questions within his compass of thinking, they received consideration and felt well paid for their efforts."

While Brother Robert was president, Prof. J. E. Stubbs, a Methodist, was vice-president, or rather acting president, for to him was given the management of the courses, matriculation of students, discipline, etc.

Brother Robert spent most of his time among the churches, working in the interest of the college. He spent much time on committees and on special calls from the churches, but wherever he went he was wielding an influence for the school. Many students were enrolled at Ashland for no other reason than that the brethren had faith in its leader. Those who were students there at the time say that the student body was always glad for his presence in chapel because of the interesting practicable and sound talks that he gave them. Some of his positions were in accord with the best pedagogical thought of today.

Even with so loyal a man at the head of the college, many were suspicious of higher education and frequently he had to correct false reports that went out concerning the school. While he understood and id not ignore the feelings of the old brethren, yet he was always firm in upholding the cause of higher education. One of his defenses in favor of the work is worth repeating:

"EDUCATION.

"We live in an age of wonderful improvement. All the arts and industries of the world make a business so great that we are struck with astonishment when reviewing the vast amount of skill and labor necessary to carry on the work and supply the wants of man as he now lives. Taking this view of it, we can see at once that the world needs something more in the line of education than simply that given in the common schools of our day.

"Without something more than a common school education, we could not even have an almanac. The common schools do not teach the science of astronomy nor compute eclipses. They do not teach the surveying that we must have. They do not teach bookkeeping; merchants need that. They do not teach engineering; every town and railroad needs that. They do not teach chemistry; the medical faculty needs that. Common schools do not teach the engineer nor direct the mariner and but very imperfectly teach the com-

## EDUCATIONAL WORK

mon branches. Those who attempt to teach the common schools now when they have never attended a higher school are doing very imperfect work.

"God is moving the world around in education and in art. In fact, all the powers that be cannot stay the progress of man in all that relates to his mind. God has made him and rules him by His power. Man cannot stand against God, nor against the great current of education that sweeps over the civilized world. If all men were farmers, if there were no business needed in the world more than is done on one of our best farms, a common school education may do; but it takes more than that to run the world.

"Again, if to make money were the greatest object of man, then a common school education may do to make fine farms and rear fine horses and cattle. But the greater object of man should be to develop his mind and spirit, in all that brings him nearer to God in wisdom and understanding. To cultivate the mind in all the works of God, all the truths of nature as well as revelation, is the design of an education. It is the design of the Creator. If a man were a mere animal, the happiness or comfort of the body is all he needs. But he is a spiritual being created in the image of God, and the full development in soul, body and spirit is the greater end for which he was created.

"If we fall behind the world in educating our children we lose our power and soon lose our children; for the education around us will, in music, science and everything that makes the knoweldge of our age, come with its influences to lead our children from us. We believe it is our duty to turn all the power that there is in an education to the glory of God and the good of his cause. Our greatest good in the world must come, not by fighting education which we cannot stop, but by turning it to the good of the world and the cause of Christianity."

In the summer of 1881 he was unanimously reëlected by the trustees as president for another year. The previous year had been the most successful year for the institution. His second year began very favorably; but the Progressive movement was growing and gradually the trustees of the colleges took a decided stand for the movement, until the majority of them were opposed to being loyal to the decisions of Annual Meeting. Brother Robert was not at all in sympathy with their position, and at their regular monthly meeting, Dec. 13, 1881, he tendered his resignation as president of the college. This was accepted and the relations existing between him and the trustees were dissolved by mutual consent with the very best of feelings. He did not quarrel with them but simply told them that he was not and could not work in sympathy with their views. During the last ten years of his life he remained a close and interested observer of the educational growth in the church.

In September, 1879, Mount Morris College was opened with J. W. Stein as president and D. L. Miller, secretary and business manager. In 1880 Spring Creek Normal School, Va., was opened by Prof. D. C. Flory, and two years later it was moved to Bridgewater, Va. In 1888 McPherson College, Kansas, began with S. Z. Sharp as president. Botetout Normal College began at Daleville Va., in 1890, with Prof. I.

## EDUCATIONAL WORK

N. H. Beahm in charge and the next year Lordsburg College, California, was started.

All of these institutions developed with varied experiences, and have since become well established schools. In addition to these at North Manchester, Ind., in Brother Robert's own congregation, three years after his death another college was founded. With none of these schools did he have any direct influence save Mt. Morris, where he did his last work by preparing a series of doctrinal sermons for the special Bible term.

## CHAPTER VI.

### Division.

A history of the Church of the Brethren or of any of her leading men during the last half of the nineteenth century would be incomplete without reference to the division that came to a head in the early eighties. However painful it may be to relate, most of the attention of the church for many years was directed toward those questions upon which the church divided.

The division extended in two directions. One faction was dissatisfied with innovations that were gradually creeping into the church. They seemed to place methods of doing work on an equality with fundamental principles. And so, when the Sunday-school method of instructing children was introduced, they were as much alarmed as if the very principle itself of instructing the children in the truths of God's Word had been denied them. It made no difference to them about the spirit of the times, or the environment in which they were placed: the methods of the fathers was the only right course to pursue.

The other faction was impatient with the slow progress which the church, through her Annual Meeting, was making in adopting new methods of work. They did not realize the fact that while many things may be lawful, it is not always expedient to try to force them too quickly upon a body of people who have, for generations, thought otherwise. They cared little about the opinion of the body of the church, but determined to go ahead whether the body could be taken along or not.

### THE OLD ORDER BRETHREN.

The first faction to leave the church is known as the Old Order Brethren. The chief sources of information concerning their grievances are the Annual Meeting Minutes and a fifty-three page pamphlet entitled " The Brethren's Reasons." The latter was published by a committee who stated in the preface that "The object and purpose of this pamphlet is to show how frequently the brethren did petition the Annual Meeting to put away the new and fast movement in the church, and to explain and set forth the reasons and grounds for producing and adopting the resolutions of August 24, 1881."

The first petition presented by the brethren dissatisfied with innovations was at the Annual Meeting held in Roanoke County, Va., in 1869. The original petition was framed at a meeting held in the Stillwater church, Ohio, November 13, 1868. It contained three grievances that the brethren desired to have corrected.

First, they objected to choosing the Standing Committee from different States " like our Representatives in Congress," and would not have the names of the committee appear on the Minutes. They wanted this committee to consist of " six or eight of the old, experienced and established brethren selected from the elders present at the place of Annual Meeting." These brethren were to receive queries and present them in order before the meeting, but no brother was to be selected as moderator, " rather submitting that office to the dictations of the Holy Spirit." Second, they objected to the Annual Meeting sending committees to settle difficulties in local churches. This work should be done by the home church, assisted by elders of adjoining congregations, while the work of Annual Meeting was to be confined to questions or ordinances and doctrine. Third, they desired more care exercised on the part of the editors and contributors of the *Gospel Visitor* and *Christian Family Companion,* that there be " nothing in their periodicals that disputes the practice of the precepts and ordinances of the Gospel as handed down to us from Christ and the apostles, through and by the forefathers of the church."

At the close of the petition a hint was given that unless the grievances were corrected a division could not long be delayed. Some of the brethren thought the petition ought to contain references to other changes from the established order. So, at a meeting held in the Bear Creek church near Dayton, Ohio, March 29, 1869, a supplement was prepared to the former petition. The purpose of the meeting as stated in the supplement was to adopt " measures consistent with the Gospel, whereby the church may be cleansed, if possible, from the doctrines and principles of the popular religion of the day, and to prevent the further introduction of said doctrines and principles into our fraternity "; also to name a few items " for the sake of those of our dear brethren who have not had the age and experience, and perhaps have never had the opportunity of becoming thoroughly acquainted with the fundamental principles of our church."

# DIVISION

The items mentioned were as follows: First, Protracted meetings. While advocating an active and industrious ministry, they objected to getting members in the church by " working upon the passions of the people, without giving them sufficient time to reflect and consider the cost." Nor did they think it right to sound through the church papers, in a half-boastful way, the success in number of additions that attended the preaching. Second, While they recognized the Christian duty of parents to teach moral and religious lessons to their children at home, they objected to Sabbath schools, which " in themselves present a very harmless and innocent appearance, but in reality their tendency is to pride and self-praise." Third, they found no Scripture authority for " Prayer meetings, social meetings and Bible classes."

The supplement goes on to show how that little by little these things had crept into the church and " that most generally where the brethren have these new orders among them, fashionable dressing and pride are a natural consequence." Other denominations had started plain but had gone worldlyward. The Brethren church was following in the same channel. She was " too grasping and contending wonderfully for an easy, pleasant and popular religion, in which there is less sacrifice and self-denial."

The Annual Meeting of 1869 treated the above petition and its supplement with due respect and gave an answer that dealt with every grievance presented. While the Conference would not do away with the things objected to, yet it did advise that the umost care be taken that all objectionable features of the innovations referred to be eliminated. This answer was far from satisfying the plaintiffs, who characterized it as a compromise at best; but it did not put off for a decade the threatened division.

During these years other questions were constantly coming up that tended still further to separate the brethren. Sunday schools, academies, protracted meetings, and the single mode of feet-washing were becoming more and more common. The progressive part of the church was taking more liberty every year. On the subject of feet-washing especially, there were many bitter disputes. "It is remarkable," says H. R. Holsinger, "that an intelligent body of such devoted people should suffer themselves to become alienated from each other in regard to the manner of observing an ordinance which was instituted for the special purpose of uniting them more closely, by inculcating the spirit of self-abnegation and humility."

When the Old Order Brethren could no longer endure the growth of what they considered contrary to the Gospel, they once more appealed to Annual Meeting. As before, the elders of Southern Ohio were in the lead. In November, 1879, most of the elders of the Miami Valley met in the Salem church and framed the famous Miami Valley Petition. Their list of grievances now included highschools, Sunday schools, protracted meetings and single-mode feet-washing. The closing appeal of these elders shows their earnestness in regard to the evils of the church as they saw them. The district meeting of Southern Ohio did not fully indorse this petition, but sent it to the Annual Meeting of 1880. The Stand-

## DIVISION

ing Committee felt the gravity of the situation and carefully framed the following answer which the Conference passed:

"Whereas, Our beloved Fraternity has been considerably disturbed by brethren holding extreme views, some being disposed to enforce more rigorously the order of the church in regard to nonconformity to the world, and the principle of nonconformity to the world in giving form to our costume, than has commonly been done by our ancient brethren; while some on the other extreme, would abandon the principle of nonconformity so far as that principle has anything to do with giving form to our costume; and

"Whereas, The principle of nonconformity in giving form to our costume, as well as in everything else, has been a peculiar characteristic of our Fraternity, and is so stated in our written history, and has had its influence with our nonswearing and noncombatant and our general principles, identifying our Fraternity with the primitive and apostolic church in preserving us from the extravagant expenditures which both the religious and secular world have fallen into, and obtaining for us as a body the character of simplicity, honesty, purity, and uprightness in the world; and

"Whereas, It is thought by many, and even so declared, that as a body we are opposed to all improvements and progress; and

"Whereas, Contention and strife in the church are great obstacles in the way of both its holiness and its usefulness; therefore

"Resolved, First, that we will labor in the spirit of the Gospel, and in brotherly love to maintain the principles of nonconformity in giving form to our costume, and in every way that the recognized peculiarities of our Fraternity require.

"Resolved, Secondly, that while we declare ourselves conservative in maintaining unchanged what may justly be considered the principles and peculiarities of our Fraternity, we also believe in the propriety and necessity of so adapting our labor and our principles to the religious wants of the world as will render our labor and principles most efficient in promoting the reformation of the world, the edification of the church and the glory of God. Hence while we are conservative, we are also progressive.

"Resolved, Thirdly, that brethren teaching through the press or ministry, or in any other way, sentiments conflicting with the recognized principles and peculiarities of our Fraternity, shall be considered offenders and be dealt with as such. And to specify more particularly the subjects named in the petition we offer the following as an answer:

"1. Inasmuch as there exists a widespread fear among us that the brethren's high schools are likely to operate against the simplicity of the Gospel of Christ, as also likely to cultivate the desire for an exclusively educated ministry; to guard, therefore, these schools from producing these effects, we think the principals of these schools should meet and adopt rules that will prevent such tendency, and said rules to be in harmony with the principles of Annual Meeting.

"2. Sabbath schools, when held in the spirit of the Gospel, may be made a means of bringing up our children in the ' nurture and admonition of the Lord.' But should have no picnics and celebrations or any vain things of the popular Sabbath schools of the day as connected with them.

" 3. All meetings for worship should be held as our stated or regular meetings are held, and we be cautious not to use such means as are calculated to get people into the church without a gospel conversion—such as over-persuasion or excitement—but use the gospel means to get them to turn away from sin.

" 4. In regard to a paid ministry, we believe that it is not right for brethren to go and labor for churches in the hope of receiving money for services, nor the offer of money as an inducement for brethren to preach; but to poor ministers, who are faithful, both in the doctrine and practice of the church, we would encourage giving toward their necessity; as also defraying the expenses of travelling in attending to church interests.

" 5 Inasmuch as our old fathers have always admitted the validity of the two modes of feet-washing, and as much as we desire a more perfect union in this matter, we cannot condemn either mode as being invalid. And inasmuch as former decisions have failed to settle this question to the satisfaction of all, we advise more forbearance and liberty to the conscience of our brethren in this matter, because both have been practiced among us, and the best way to stop the agitation of this question is to allow the same liberty of conscience for our brethren that we ask for ourselves. But this shall not be construed to annul the present decision and advice of Annual Meeting."

This reply was far from satisfactory to those who

had sent the petition. The fact that the Conference attempted to throw safeguards around various institutions availed nothing; for, in the eyes of the plaintiffs, the Annual Meeting, by this very act, acknowledged the legal existence of these things in the church. They now saw that the single mode of feet-washing had come to stay. Two expressions of the report were especially offensive: First, "The best way to stop the agitation of this question is to allow the same liberty of conscience for our brethren that we ask for ourselves"; and second, "While we are conservative, we are also progressive." Liberty of conscience and progression were two expressions intolerable to them. They were also seriously opposed to taking and printing a full report of the Annual Meeting.

The Southern Ohio brethren resolved to make one more attempt to get their desires recognized by the Conference. They called a meeting, to convene in the Wolf Creek church, December 8, 1880. To this meeting all the "faithful and steadfast brethren—both in the ministry and at the visit—who are in favor of the ancient and apostolic order of the church, as set forth in said petition, are most heartily invited."

The meeting was held at the time appointed. Many prominent brethren from different States were present. A series of resolutions were passed and sent to Annual Meeting. These resolutions demanded that single mode feet-washing, Sunday schools, protracted meetings, high schools, paid ministry and organized missionary work be at once put away. In short, nothing would satisfy them but for Annual Meeting to declare illegal every change of the last thirty years.

## DIVISION 103

The result was such as might have been expected. The Annual Meeting of 1881 refused to yield to the demands and readopted the decision of 1880 regarding the Miami Valley petition. It was now evident that the Old Order Brethren could expect nothing more from Annual Meeting and the only means of securing their own way was to separate entirely from the church. After due announcement, a meeting was held in the Ludlow and Painter Creek church, near Arcanum, Ohio, August 24, 1881. A large congregation was present and after much deliberation, the meeting passed the following paper which reviewed their grievances, set forth their principles and outlined their future policy.

"Dear Brethren: It is manifest that our church is in a confused condition, and that duty requires something to be done for the peace and union of the church. There is a spirit or element among us that is disturbing our peace. Our dear old brethren have borne it all patiently for about thirty years. Up to the year 1851, peace and union existed in the church. In the year 1851, the first paper was granted to be printed amongst us. In 1857, Sunday schools were rather granted; in 1858 liberty was also granted for long revival meetings and also high schools. These somewhat disturbed the peace of many brethren. Thus we see clearly that when the order of the church was once broken, one new innovation and deviation after another crept in amongst us to the sorrow of many brethren and sisters.

"Two ways of observing the ordinances of the house of God also crept in amongst us, greatly disturbing the peace of the church. First, the supper was put on the table at the time of feet-washing. After a little some also wanted the bread and wine on the table at the same time. And now also two or three ways are suffered in practicing the ordinance of feet-washing. And the single mode is also strongly advocated and was very nearly granted by the Annual Meeting of 1880. Money soliciting and begging is also granted, and what next the Lord only knows.

"Dear brethren, do we not clearly see that we are fast drifting into the popular customs of the world? Thus far our old brethren have suffered themselves to be led along until they feel to be led no farther in this current. So far they have borne all these things patiently, but have made many efforts by sending query after query to Annual Meeting, which accomplished but little in checking this fast element among us. A mild and friendly petition was sent to the Annual Meeting of 1880, praying that body to grant the request therein asked for. But instead of that they framed an unsatisfactory substitute with an answer. After a close investigation of that substitute and answer, many brethren considered it to be unscriptural, and we think it has been a cause of divisions in the church. Many brethren and sisters were, therefore, not satisfied with it, and so we sent it to the Annual Meeting again in 1881, when it was rejected and made out illegal together with the council of December 8, 1880. Many tender feelings were wounded in looking over these proceedings, and hence are discouraged in making any further efforts or requests to this body, which, of late years has been so much controlled by the fast element that it looks as if the old brethren are but little regarded.

"Now, dear brethren, you need not wonder or fault us, when we feel to be led no further in this popular current, and hence have made this another effort in calling a council to effect something for the peace and union of our church, to try and agree upon some rule or order for the Brethren church in the future. And we see no safer plan than to adhere more strictly to the ancient order of the church as practiced by the ancient fathers of our church, which we believe was in strict harmony with the spirit of the Gospel, and in which a number of our churches were organized in the same faith once delivered to the saints, and hence about all believed in the universal practice of our ancient brethren with few exceptions.

"Be it therefore resolved, That we will more strictly adhere to the self-denying principles of the Gospel. as practiced by our ancient brethren and as set forth in our petition of 1880, to which we wish to hold. With this amendment, as the petition mentions popular Sunday schools and revival meetings the way they are generally conducted, to be more clearly understood, we say that we feel to suffer none in the Brethren church and then we will be sure to have no trouble with them. No Sunday schools, no high schools, no revival meetings, no paid ministry, no missionary plans or mission boards, as now granted by Annual Meeting. No money soliciting or begging to carry out such plans. No single mode of feet-washing, no musical instruments, as pianos, melodeons, and organs. No unlawful interest to oppress the poor.

"Resolved further, that we fully adhere to primitive Christianity as taught by Christ and his apostles in all his commandments and precepts, as practiced by our forefathers. And we strictly adhere to a plain and decent uniformity of dress as soldiers of King Immanuel. That the brethren wear a plain round-breasted coat with a standing collar; hat, overcoat and everything else to correspond. A plain way of wearing the hair and beard, no fashionable mustaches and no roached or shingled hair. The sisters also to wear a plain modest dress and bonnet; also a plain white cap in time of worship or on going abroad. In short that the brethren and sisters let their light shine as a light on a 'candlestick,' and not part or wholly under the 'bushel,' but to show to the world that we try to possess what we profess. And above all that the brethren and sisters be more or their guard and more reserved in their conversation, as that unruly tongue is doing much mischief among us.

"Now the above named things we claim are in strict harmony with the spirit of the Gospel and thus we should strictly adhere to and fulfill our baptismal vow which we made before God and many witnesses. Also, we look upon our many periodicals, the way they are conducted, as being very injurious to the cause of our Master.

"We are by no means opposed to mission work if carried out in gospel order. Neither are we opposed to assist our poor ministers in such work. And when we speak of carrying out the ancient order of our church, we do not mean all little usages and customs that were amongst our people. But to be more of

## DIVISION

'one mind' and speak and teach more the one and same thing as taught by the apostles.

"Now after this resolution is accepted, we advise that all our members be counciled in every church in the valley, and in all other districts in our Brotherhood that unite with us. And we advise that two faithful and impartial elders be present at those councils, as we want nothing but honesty and fairness. But just before any council is gone into, the members should be well instructed and enlightened in every point, showing no partiality nor forbidding brethren to give their opinion in love on both sides. After the members are well enlightened, let each member express his own mind that a fair decision may be made; so we can learn how many will stand united to the ancient order of the church. And if some should ask time to consider, let it be granted. To such the door of the church is open. But such as will express themselves not willing to stand united with the ancient order of our church, we cannot help them, and if they will afterwards change their minds and wish to unite with us, they will then have to enter legally according to order. The door of the church to be open to them also. But such as will not stand united with us in the apostolic order of our church, will then have to be disfellowshipped from the Old Brethren's church."

These resolutions were signed by fifteen elders. The movement spread rapidly but the division was not effected peacefully. Those who accepted the resolutions were very soon disfellowshipped from the churches of Southern Ohio. The Annual Meeting of 1882 recognized the legality of these expulsions. The reasons complain bitterly the way old and faithful brethren and sisters were excommunicated. But it is difficult to see what other course was open. The Old Order Brethren were most intolerant themselves and fully intended, wherever they could, to disown all who would not agree with them. In many places congregations were very evenly divided and there much conflict arose, especially over the possession of church property. The fact is that on both sides many things were said and done that were better left unrecorded.

At a meeting held in the barn of Abraham Landis, in the bounds of the Salem church, Montgomery County, Ohio, the new organization took the name of Old German Baptist Brethren and arrangements were made for a general conference. Large numbers were joining them all over the country. In all, about three thousand were thus lost to the Conservatives. At their first Annual Meeting, held at Brookville, Ohio, in 1882, congregations were represented from nine different States. These meetings have been held yearly ever since on Pentecost. The questions brought and the manner of their decisions show that the church is still that of the nonprogressive, Old Order Brethren. After the division movement had spent its force, their numbers ceased to increase and at present they are gradually decreasing.

### THE PROGRESSIVE BRETHREN.

The division in the Church of the Brethren furnishes us an interesting example of how far apart honest men may come to differ in their opinions. We have just seen how worldly and fast the Old Order Brethren considered the Annual Meeting to be. At the same time the Progressive Brethren thought this same conference to be, beyond all reason, too slow in making changes.

The Progressive movement largely centers around one man, H. R. Holsinger, who was more responsible than any other one man for the division. In his history of the Tunkers and Brethren church, he has given a very complete, though naturally a somewhat one-sided account of the various steps that led to the division. In introducing his account Holsinger says: "With the appearance of the *Gospel Visitor,* 1851, was ushered in the progressive era of the Tunker church. It was so prophesied by its opposers, and we must do them the honor of stating that they were true prophets in each case." As stated elsewhere, Holsinger served for a time as an assistant on the *Gospel Visitor,* but believing in a more progressive and a weekly paper, he began publishing the *Christian Family Companion* in 1864.

There were many things in the church, as Holsinger saw it, that were very irritating to him. He believed that the ministry of the church ought to be better educated. Especially was it wrong that so much power be concentrated in the hands of ignorant elders, many of whom, he declares, could scarcely read a chapter in the Bible intelligently. Then too, order in dress and church ritual was everywhere insisted upon while many of the vital questions of the day were scarcely noticed.

In his new paper, Holsinger adopted the policy of a free rostrum for the discussion of all subjects pertaining to the work of the church. He believed that the church was in need of great reformation and was not slow in giving his views in his editorials. It is no wonder that much opposition was stirred up, some of which was very inconsistent, especially in the light of the present practice of the church. Many of the things for which Holsinger contended have long since been sanctioned by Annual Meeting. Had he only been more considerate in his method of presenting his views, he might have more easily convinced the brethren and thus avoided the division later.

At the conference of 1867, in Carroll County, Md., he raised quite a commotion by insisting on what he considered the gospel method of setting apart deacons instead of the established order of the church. Again, in 1869, he was much censured for trying to force a reporter upon Annual Meeting. He was hasty and plain out with his thoughts, both in speech and writing; and so there was no end of his trouble with the brethren who sincerely felt that his teachings were a great menace to the welfare of the church.

Holsinger himself became tired of being at variance continually with the brethren and he felt that as long as he was editing a church paper he had to speak his convictions. So he sought an interview with Elder James Quinter, editor of the *Gospel Visitor,* and offered to sell to him. Elder Quinter accepted the proposition and combined the two papers. The free rostrum was now eliminated, for Elder Quinter, while believing in some reforms, was much more conservative in the method of advocating them.

In the fall of 1878, Holsinger in connection with J. W. Beer, started the *Progressive Christian* at Berlin,

Pa., "with the avowed purpose of advocating progressive measures and reforms." It was through this paper that Holsinger came into a determined conflict with Annual Meeting, which finally led to his expulsion and the organization of the Progressive Brethren church.

As a result of several queries sent by several State districts to the Annual Meeting of 1879, Holsinger and some contributors to his paper were required to make satisfaction for certain schismatic articles that had appeared in the *Progressive Christian*. The conference also attempted to throw safeguards around all the various church papers by appointing a committee whose duty it was to see that these periodicals admitted no articles that would disturb the peace of the church.

Elder J. W. Beer now felt that the paper should be run in a more conservative way, but Holsinger objected, and later sold out his interest to the senior editor. Elder Beer soon found the business an unpaying one and stopped the paper. In May, 1880, it was revived by Howard Miller and H. R. Holsinger, the latter soon becoming sole proprietor and editor. The policy of the paper was henceforth radically progressive. Schismatic articles appeared in the editorial columns and the essay department. Great alarm was felt by the conservative brethren everywhere, and in 1881 there were no less than five petitions presented by State districts to the Annual Meeting at Ashland, Ohio.

The report of this year shows that the session was a stormy one. After a long discussion a committee was appointed to wait on Elder Holsinger in his home church. This committee, consisting of John Wise, Enoch Eby, David Long, Joseph Kauffman and Christian Bucher, is known as the Berlin Committee. What the result of their work was can best be gleaned from their report to the Annual Meeting, held at Milford, Ind., May 30, 1882:

"We, the undersigned committee, appointed by Annual Meeting to go to the Berlin church, Somerset County, Pa., to wait on Elder H. R. Holsinger, and deal with him according to his transgressions, do report as follows:

"Met with the Berlin church on Tuesday, August 9, 1881, and were unanimously accepted by the church, H. R. Holsinger included. And upon the question to H. R. Holsinger, whether he would accede to, and accept of, the general usages of the church in conducting this investigation, he declined, whereupon a lengthy discussion followed upon the following departure from the general usages of the church:

"1st, H. R. Holsinger employed a stenographer to take down and publish the proceedings of the council. 2nd, The council to be held in the presence of persons not members of the church, which discussion closed by the Berlin church saying that they had passed a resolution in the absence of the committee, that they will have a full report of proceedings taken; and right on this, passed, in the presence of the committee, the following:

"'Resolved that this council shall be held openly to all members, and persons not members of the Brethren church will be considered present by courtesy only, and none but the members of the Berlin church and the committee are invited to participate in the business.'

"Wednesday, August 10, met at 9 A. M. according to adjournment. The chairman announced to the meeting that the committee feared that the members did not understand the responsibilities they assumed yesterday and proposed a reconsideration and rescinding of their decisions. After some investigation of the propriety of reconsideration Brother Holsinger gave liberty for any one to make a motion to that effect, but no motion was offered. After due time the committee retired and decided as follows:

"'In view of the above considerations, especially in view of the fact that Brother H. R. Holsinger refused to have his case investigated by the committee in harmony with the Gospel as interpreted by Annual Meeting, and the consent of our general Brotherhood, and inasmuch as Brother H. R. Holsinger and the Berlin church assumed all responsibility in the case, therefore we decided: that Brother H. R. Holsinger cannot be held in fellowship in the Brotherhood and all who depart with him shall be held responsible to the action of the next Annual Meeting.'"

It is doubtful if any other Annual Meeting of the Church of the Brethren was ever awaited with such fearful forebodings as the one of 1882. Elder Holsinger and those who sympathized with him did not consider the work of the committee legal, while many who did not sympathize with him felt that the committee had overstepped its bounds. On the other hand, the majority of the church felt that patience with Elder Holsinger had ceased to be a virtue and that the decision of the committee was the best thing possible under the circumstances. In the meantime, Elder Holsinger continued his work as a minister and bishop; and as an editor he was never more active than during these months following his expulsion by the committee. Many articles appeared in the *Progressive Christian* from his friends, who vigorously lampooned the committee for their action. This only caused the situation to become more intense and all looked forward to see whether the Annual Meeting would accept the report of the committee.

After the above report was read at Arnold's Grove, Elder John Wise made an explanation of their work and gave reasons both from the Minutes of Annual Meeting and the Gospel to uphold the course of the committee. D. C. Moomaw then presented what he termed the Olive Branch of Peace. According to this, Elder Holsinger was to make satisfaction for his past offenses, and promise to conduct himself in the future in harmony with the doctrine and practices of the church. In order that this paper might be examined by Holsinger's friends before they endorsed it, Brother Moomaw desired that final decision be put off till the next day.

Following this, a heated discussion began and continued during most of the day. Holsinger's friends, and even many who had been his greatest opponents, contended that he ought to have one more chance to set himself right. Others believed that the time for this was past until the Conference had accepted the report of the committee; then if Elder Holsinger was sincere in his desire to work with the church, he could be reinstated at any time in the regular way. He, however, said that while he could acknowledge to Annual Meeting that he had made mistakes, he could never acknowledge that the work of that committee was legal. When the motion to accept the committee's report was put to the meeting, it was declared adopted. " In those days all the members present voted. When the question was put the six thousand present seemed to arise en masse in favor of the report; not over two hundred stood against it."

Immediately after the report of the Berlin committee was accepted, a meeting was arranged for by Holsinger's friends to consider what steps should be taken. This meeting met at a schoolhouse one mile west of the Conference ground. Elder P. J. Brown was chairman. A resolution of sympathy was extended to H. R. Holsinger. A petition addressed to the Standing Committee was drawn up to the effect that another effort be made to effect a reconciliation and prevent another division in the church. The Standing Committee refused to consider this petition on the ground that it had not come in the proper way through a district meeting.

A division, such as the Old Order Brethren had effected some nine months before, was now decided upon. A series of resolutions was passed and a convention was called to be held at Ashland, Ohio, June 29, 1882. At this convention, delegates from many States were present. A declaration of principles was adopted. In this their principles were set forth, the abuses and errors of the mother church were recited, their own efforts for reform were given, and finally a resolution was made that they had not seceded, but were the true conservators of the Brethren church that had been organized in Germany in 1708.

It was further agreed that a general convention should be held only when necessary. A committee was appointed to make efforts to consolidate with various kindred denominations known as Congregational Brethren, Leedy Brethren, River Brethren, Conservative Brethren and Shoemaker Brethren. Another committee was appointed to reconstruct and organize churches. It is estimated that about six thousand five hundred members left the old mother church, to go with the progressive movement. Their numbers have slowly increased. The first general convention was held at Dayton, Ohio, June 7, 1883. Here the name, "The Brethren Church," was adopted as their church name.

The Brethren Church now began its career as a separate institution. The Publishing House at Ashland, Ohio, and the college at the same place were both controlled by trustees, the majority of whom were in sympathy with progressive ideas, and so passed into the hands of the new organization. The second general convention was held at Ashland, Ohio, September 21, 1887, and the third at Warsaw, Ind., August 23, 1892. Since then the conference has met almost yearly.

---

In this account of the division, we have seemingly lost sight of the subject of this biography. But not so. The history of the division is inseparably connected with events in the life of Elder R. H. Miller. Not that he fostered division; but on the contrary he was one of the strongest advocates of submission to the decisions of Annual Meeting. He was prominent in the church during the entire trouble.

His first service on the Standing Committee was in 1869, when the Old Order Brethren presented their first list of grievances. During the next ten years he was often called upon to uphold the decisions of Annual Meeting in committee work, in the pulpit, in the church papers and by private influence. His first and only service as moderator of Annual Meeting was in 1879, when the great outburst of feeling against the progressive element came in from several State districts. He was present at the meeting in the Wolf Creek church, December, 1880, and together with Elder James Quinter and others attempted to temper the radical views of the Old Order Brethren. For the next year he was in the very heart of the radical progressive element at Ashland, Ohio, where, as president of the college and editor of the *Gospel Preacher,* he was constantly face to face with troublesome problems. It was through the columns of the *Preacher* that his strongest defenses of Annual Meeting were made. His views can best be set forth by quotations from a few of his best articles:

"SOME THINGS MAGNIFIED.

"There is often a difference in the views of men in the church about small things which would, in themselves, do little harm to the peace of the church. A little difference may be badly managed and result in as great troubles as if it were the most essential matter. To differ quietly and peaceably about matters of little importance, or those not essential, will seldom do any harm. But to begin writing and making public every matter of difference, contending over it, will soon magnify it into something dangerous to the welfare of the church. Many small matters of difference would die out if they were let alone, but when they are made a bone of contention, they grow to such proportions that they soon destroy the peace of the church.

"Most of the troubles in our church today are of this kind; the points of difference, mainly, existed forty years ago, and even from the beginning. Then there was little said about them and that was in kindness. Now there is much said, and some of it is far from being in kindness. To illustrate, take the subject of dress. We cannot remember the time when there was not some difference in that. But once there was little said and no contention over it. Now there are many things written, that tend to magnify that difference, spread it wider and deeper and higher, till the spirit of union and peace our fathers had seems to be lost in the midst of a strife that has been no real benefit to any one, but a great loss to the church, and if continued will result in division.

"There is but one remedy and that is to follow the example of our fathers; compromise and reconcile all minor differences in a council like Annual Meeting, and then abide by it until it can be made better by the same council."—*Gospel Preacher, Vol. I, Page. 258.*

## "DISSENSION.

"At this time we have two dissenting elements in our Brotherhood. One extreme wishes to break down the established order in some of our practices. They do so because they dissent from the order. They are called Progressives; but that is the wrong name because it gives the wrong idea. They want to break down the established order of plainness in the church. Progression means to build something up and make it stronger; dissension means to turn from it or against it. Dissenters is the right name because it gives the idea that they are against the order established by the Annual Conference.

"Another class of brethren dissent from the Annual Conference, because it assumes the right to reconsider and change its own decision in some matters that they do not want to see changed. They also dissent from Annual Meeting because she will not change the decisions and make some things a test of fellowship which were not made so before; such as the single mode of feet-washing and the form of apparel. These dissensions against the authority of Annual Meeting is the cause of troubles. When these dissensions become parties, led by public journals, we cannot reasonably look for any other result than division, or the dissenters going off if they cannot rule.

"This result is more sad because it will produce no good to the church or the world. If the fast dissenters could break down our order of plainness, and get the church just like the world in that particular, neither the church nor the world would be made better by it;

neither would any truth of the Gospel be made stronger. There are enough of the churches now going with the world in pride and fashion. We cannot gain anything but strife and division, by the effort to break down the order of plainness in the church. Some will tell us they do not want to break down the plainness of the church. It is presumption to talk of maintaining plainness if we break down the established order. There is not a church in the Brotherhood that maintains the order of plainness if it has set aside the uniformity given in the Annual Conference; because just as soon as the uniformity sustained by the Annual Meeting is lost, the dissenters turn the other way. Thus one step after another is taken until all the world has in fashionable dress is worn by the sisters and probably by the brethren. This is the result of dissension in that particular as we have seen in every case where the cause is allowed to exist.

"These parties, made by this dissension from the general Brotherhood, are deceiving the church to a great extent; the progressives by assuming a good name, by assuming that all improvement and advancement in doing good in the church is progressive and that it is their work. Now the truth is, the good work has been done by those who are in favor of the order of the church. The Denmark mission was commenced by them. The missionary work and plans we now have, were made by them. The district organizations in missionary work were made by brethren who labor to sustain the established order of the church. As it is in missionary work so it is in Sabbath school, education, and series of meetings; they are the work of those who maintain the order of the church. Some of the dissenters on the one side are trying to do things the conference never sanctioned; on the other side they oppose and refuse to do things it has sanctioned. Both of these parties led on by public journals, will, if continued, certainly produce division, for it is the child of dissension."—*Gospel Preacher, Vol. I, page 414.*

Thus it may be seen that Brother Robert was bold and fearless in opposing the policy of both the Old Order Brethren and the Progressive Brethren. But in so doing he cherished no bitter feeling in his heart toward them. His charity was as broad as his intellectual grasp of the church's problems or his loyalty to her decisions. Concerning the Old Order Brethren after they had decided to leave he wrote:

" We have received several letters asking about what is the proper course to pursue, in those churches where some have gone off with the Old Order, on the petition gotten up in the Miami Valley. We have always advised caution and kindness to be observed in every case of expulsion, when it is possible. Many will go off with the Old Order, who are honest, good-meaning brethren; we would advise such a course to be taken that it would hold their good will if possible, and leave the best of feeling under the circumstances. A Christian spirit should be shown in every case and erring brethren be looked upon with all the charity their case will allow. All should be treated as brethren until they are expelled legally, and afterwards they should be treated with kindness."

On the other hand he was equally charitable toward H. R. Holsinger and his friends. At Arnold's Grove, he opposed hasty action in accepting the report of the Berlin committee. In one of his speeches he said; " Let us get at, if we can, our true responsibility to God and before the world for our action. Think of the principles involved in our conduct and you have a matter of importance. This is a peculiar case of the trial of a brother that occurred in a very peculiar manner. The report has come here against that brother condemning him. You have heard the report; and on top of that report, before the brother was even heard at all, a motion was made that the report be accepted. We were asked to accept the report without hearing the brother at all. I have been against that brother more than anyone else in the Brotherhood. And though I have been against him often, and contended with him long and much, yet today I am not ready to vote until that brother, who has been condemned in the report, has an opportunity to be heard. He has not been heard. Hence I favor the motion to give him all the time he asks to make a full answer; and after we have heard him, we will decide whether we will accept this report or not."

Eld. Jas. Quinter, Pa.
Secretary of A M

Eld. D P. Sayler, Md.
Moderator A. M.

Eld. R. H. Miller, Ind.
Announced Organization A. M.

LEADERS OF ANNUAL MEETING, 1877

## CHAPTER VII.

### ANNUAL MEETING.

Next to the Bible, Elder R. H. Miller held that the Annual Meeting was the highest authority to direct the church and the actions of individual members. Whatever might have been his own beliefs, which he always defended in the councils with great ability, yet when a decision was once made, he submissively yielded his own opinions until he had another opportunity in the same council to get decisions changed to what he considered right. A few brethren may have had as much formative influence on the decisions of Annual Meeting as he; but when once the decision was made, it is not too much to say that the church never had a man who so ably defended the positions of Annual Meeting as Elder R. H. Miller. His views on the position and function of Annual Meeting can best be learned from his own words:

"Some brethren have held that Annual Meeting is a legislative body. That is not correct. They might just as well call a council meeting a legislative body. The Annual Meeting and all church meetings are judiciary, merely as a court to decide upon all questions brought before it. The Annual Meeting has no power to originate bills and pass them as laws; but hear the case brought up from a local council, or District Meeting and decide it as a supreme court would do. Its decisions are to our Brotherhood, as the decisions of the supreme court to the citizens of the United States; not a congress to make laws, but a court to decide according to laws already made. So our Annual Meeting decides the case brought before it, according to the Gospel—the law God has made for the government of his church. All these cases that come up must be decided by somebody. Either each individual must decide for himself—that would be individualism; or each local church must decide it—that would be congregationalism; or each District Meeting must decide for itself—that would be division at once on the principle of State rights; or the Annual Meeting must decide it according to the 15th of Acts.

"The church must have a rule, an order to govern it in everything. A ship on the ocean without a compass, without a mariner, carried by the wind and waves is soon wrecked and lost; so with the church without rule and order. Without God's Word and hand to direct its cause, it will soon drift with the current of fashion into all the ways of the world, and be lost in that vortex where there is no real difference between the church and the world. Many of the rules laid down in the Gospel are contrary to the carnal mind, but they are in perfect harmony with the spiritual mind when their object is fully understood. Though it is sad to see those who are not willing to be governed by the general order of the Brotherhood, given up to the world, yet we believe the church does right in separating from them. Because it is a truth plain to all men, that when a man belongs to a church, or any organization, and will not submit to its rules, and obey its general order, he ought to go out, because he can only cause division and trouble by staying in."

For twenty years he never missed an Annual Meeting and was a leading character in all of these conferences. There was not one of the many questions that came up for discussion but what he was ready to express his views upon, with the purpose of helping to decide it to the best interest of the church. He was a prominent member of nearly every important committee appointed to formulate plans and decisions upon which the General Conference could act. The work of these committees has had a lasting influence upon the history of the church. In the Conference itself, he was a power. Seldom did he become confused, but often by his cool-headedness, while others were excited, he helped to clear up the question for his brethren. This he did by critically and technically examining every point in the query presented. His clear arguments and simple words generally had their effect upon the decision. He was very resourceful in putting a motion in such a form that it would meet the desires of the Conference.

He was not the first to speak, but when he did speak, it was with power. Here, as in debate, his arguments were clearly and logically presented. When he finished, little remained to be said from his point of view. It has been said that he could present his side of the argument the strongest and yield the least to his opponent of any man in the Conference. Those who differed from him had to meet his arguments before they could expect a decision in their favor. He did not always secure a decision to his liking, but he knew how to submit gracefully to the will of the majority. While he had advanced ideas on most subjects, he recognized the fact that some changes must wait till their appointed time. Unless it was a clear case that a change was right and for the best, he opposed it. His argument was that there can be no danger in staying awhile longer by the ways of the fathers, while there may be great danger in making a change before the proper time.

In the following pages we are giving a brief survey of some of the most prominent questions that were before the Conference in his day. He took an active part in discussing them and was in harmony with all the decisions, excepting one or two. He was a strong defender of the position that the church always took on such questions as war, temperance, secret societies, missionary and educational work. Some of the most important subjects have been discussed in other chapters.

### FEET-WASHING.

The manner of observing the ordinance of feet-washing was one of the chief differences that caused the Old Order Brethren to leave the church. The general custom of the church for years had been the so-called double mode. This was performed by one member washing the feet of an indefinite number, and another member wiping the feet of those washed. Then two other members would continue the work as long as they desired. In practice, however, one member did not usually wash the feet of more than two or three. There were brethren in some places who felt that this mode was not in accordance with the command of the Savior to "wash one another's feet"; nor was it in harmony with the example of the early church fathers in this country. Brother A. H. Cassel, the church antiquarian, maintained that the fathers of the early church in America generally practiced the single mode.

When this mode began to be revived, there was much opposition to it. Many were the requests that were presented to Annual Meeting to stop the custom. This body at first refused to recognize the single mode, but the custom spread so rapidly that in 1877, Annual Meeting, while affirming that the double mode was the order of the general Brotherhood, decided to bear with those churches that wished to observe the single mode, wherever it could be done unanimously and without giving trouble or offense. In following years, as queries came up on the question, the Annual Meeting always referred to its decision of 1877. The single mode gained in favor until it became the order of the general Brotherhood.

### REBAPTISM.

The Annual Meeting has often considered the question of accepting as members of the church, without rebaptism, those who have been baptized by trine immersion in other denominations. Before 1848 this privilege was granted, as the Minutes of 1838 clearly show. In 1848, however, it was considered best not to receive anyone without rebaptism. Since then queries have come up time and again asking that the early decision of the church be reaffirmed; but the Annual Meeting has steadily held to the decision of 1848.

### BREAKING OF BREAD BY THE SISTERS.

For more than fifty years this question has been before the Brotherhood. In 1857 the following query was sent to Annual Meeting: " Why do not the sisters break the bread and pass the cup to each other, in the same manner as the brethren do, at the communion? Ans.—Man being the head of the woman; and it having been the practice of the church from time immemorial, for the officiating brethren to break the bread to the sisters, we know of no scriptural reason for making a change in our practice." The next request for a change came up in 1879, but was not granted. Since then the question has been kept before the church almost continuously. In 1900 an unexpected turn in the question came when a committee reported in favor of the administrator breaking the bread to brethren and sisters alike. After one year's consideration the report was rejected. In 1909 another committee brought in a similar report which is now on the list of deferred papers for the coming conference.

### LIFE INSURANCE.

In 1883 Brother Robert made one of his greatest speeches against granting the privilege of life insurance to members of the church. The privilege had been asked before then and frequently since, but the church does not give its consent.

### ELECTION BY THE MAJORITY.

The plan of electing church officials by the majority vote, which the church has never accepted, proposes that if no brother receives a majority at first, the election is to be held by ballot, and the voting counted upon an open reading of the ballots. By limiting successive ballots to those who secure the highest number, an election by a majority is finally reached. Brother Robert strongly opposed this method for the following reasons: First, if the Holy Spirit is our Guide, he will direct the church aright in its voting. If the voting is very much scattered it shows that the church is not ready for an election, and it should be declared off. Second, to try it again virtually says to the Holy Spirit that it hasn't directed rightly. Third, when two or three are put forward, then the members not only vote for some one but they also vote against some one. Fourth, those who are elected on the plurality plan are made the unanimous choice of the church by being received by the membership.

### SUNDAY SCHOOLS.

The privilege of holding Sunday schools was first granted by the Annual Meeting in 1857. Though there was much opposition on the part of the Old Order Brethren, this decision was never repealed; but the advice was given that even where a majority was in favor of Sunday schools they should not overrule the minority in a way that showed no regard for their feelings. In 1886 a query was brought up asking that a minority should not hinder a Sunday school when two-thirds of the church was in favor of it. Here Brother Robert surprised many by strongly opposing the paper. In his own large congregation, nearly one-third was opposed to Sunday schools. He argued that to force a Sunday school upon those members would destroy the peace and happiness of his church. He believed in Sunday schools, but considered it best for those in favor to try and bring those opposed in favor with the work, and then no discord would result. Though he made one of his strongest appeals, the paper was passed. He then willingly submitted, and when he went home he told his members that they would organize a Sunday school. The old brethren, pleased with the stand their leader had taken, submitted and little trouble was ever made over the innovation.

Brother Robert never claimed to be enthusiastic over the Sunday school. He fully recognized the importance of teaching the young, but thought the better method was that of the early church fathers who gave the first, and an important part of every regular service, to instruction and singing, especially suitable to the children.

### MANDATORY DECISION.

When dissatisfaction arose in the church concerning some customs, one of the most common complaints was that the church was placing too much stress upon the decisions of Annual Meeting. Many claimed that these decisions were for advice only, and that it was not right to make obedience to them a test of fellowship. There is no doubt but that the early brethren considered many decisions binding; but as innovators became radical they refused to listen longer. Because of this the Annual Meeting of 1882 passed the so-called Mandatory Decision, which made the decisions binding upon all.

There was much complaint about the passage of this query and the next year there were papers from nine State districts asking for a repeal or a modification. After careful consideration the following answer was framed and passed:

"All queries sent to Annual Meeting for decision, shall, in all cases, be decided according to the Scriptures, where there is any direct 'Thus saith the Lord' applying to the question, and all questions to which there is no express scripture applying, shall be decided according to the spirit and meaning of the scripture, and that decision shall be the rule for all of the churches for such cases as the decisions cover; and all members who will hinder or oppose such decision shall be held as not hearing the church and shall be dealt with accordingly. The decision shall not be so construed as to prevent the Annual Meeting from giving advice, when it deems it proper to do so, and that given as advice, shall be so entered upon the Minutes."

On this question Brother Robert spoke with no uncertain sound. His speech is here quoted because it deals with a question that has been much in dispute: "I wish to make an explanation, and it is, that this answer does not repeal the mandatory act. It simply takes the word mandatory out, and leaves the principle remaining in the decision. Now if we look at this subject a moment as we should, we will see that our brethren in the past have made mandatory decisions. If we go back and look at the facts in regard to the decisions of Annual Meeting for a century we will find it to be a settled truth that Annual Meeting has always passed decisions that were held as mandatory by the Brotherhood. Annual Meeting decided that our brethren should not hold slaves; that was mandatory, and always was held so. It has decided that they should not run distilleries, and that was mandatory. It decided that they should not bear arms, and that was mandatory. It decided that brethren should not belong to secret societies, such as Free Masons, Odd Fellows, etc., and that was mandatory. That was our old fathers' belief before us, and those decisions which were not clearly expressed in God's Word they held as mandatory; and when this mandatory act is passed upon the same principle it is declaring that the government of this meeting shall be in harmony with the decisions that we have always been passing. But while our fathers passed mandatory decisions they also at the same time assumed the right to give advice, and did give it. These principles have been in our church for ages past, and this answer today reaffirms and establishes what has always been among us from the beginning of our Annual Councils. It differs but little from the mandatory act. It comes up and reaffirms or establishes that binding authority to the decisions of Annual Meeting in all its councils, and it then comes up after they are made and says we shall have authority to give advice when we deem it wise to do so; it gives us authority both to pass mandatory decisions and to give advice. That was not in the mandatory clause last year, and upon that point there was considerable confusion. In this answer on that point there can be none, and it was made to avoid that. Brethren, when you talk about repealing the mandatory power of Annual Meeting, when you ask that to be passed because some few districts desire it repealed, you will find it cannot really be done at all, and you pull down the work of our fathers for a century that has gone by. No government worthy the name of government will pass mandatory decisions to govern its subjects or members, and then tell them they can do as they please. But I arose only to make an explanation. Our fathers said that the decisions of Annual Meeting were advisory. They did it because they lived in a day, thank God, when the advice of our Annual Meeting to the Brotherhood was strong enough; when faith, love and union were so deep in the hearts of the members of the church, that advice was enough. When they heard it they would take it. Now we come down to this day of trial and trouble and anxiety, and the advice of Annual Meeting has been treated as the wind. Brethren have said, ' It is only advice, and we will take it if we choose, and we will let it go if we choose.' Now when that came to be the case we had to change this matter a little. We had to have something that would meet the case of those who say they will not be submissive to the advice of Annual Meeting. We had to have a decision that would permit us to enforce the government of the church handed down by our fathers. It takes mandatory acts to put down this spirit of rebellion, this spirit of ambition and warfare against the Brotherhood. We must pass this decision."

## PLANS OF HOLDING ANNUAL MEETING.

Different plans of conducting the Annual Meeting have been in use at different times. Until 1851 a love feast was always held on Sunday evening before the conference was to begin. This custom was dropped when the attendance became too large. One or two delegates were sent from each church. These were divided into a number of subcommittees, to which were assigned the various queries that they might be put in shape to be presented to the open conference. The Standing Committee was made up of elders present, and were chosen by the bishops of the congregation and adjoining congregations in which the Annual Meeting was held. This plan was changed in 1868 when the district meeting began selecting the members on the Standing Committee. Many changes were made in 1866 on recommendation of a committee of which D. P. Saylor was foreman. The delegate body was to be composed of the elders present and a delegate sent by each district meeting. Meetings were to be held on Sunday in the neighborhood of the Annual Meeting grounds, but none on the grounds. Tuesday after Pentecost was set as the day to open the Council. The present officers of Annual Meeting were provided for, while the former subcommittees of delegates were abandoned.

It was further decided to retain the old custom of entertaining privately, free of charge, those who were in attendance. This placed a great burden upon the members of the congregations where the meeting was held. In 1879 a committee, of which R. H. Miller was chairman, advised a change so that each brother who attended should pay one dollar and the sisters could pay what they desired. The conference accepted the report, and in a few years it was willing to make the charges even greater.

In 1876 the permission was given to publish in book form the full report of Annual Meeting. Before this the papers had published synopses of speeches but the names of speakers were not given. In 1882 it was decided that the delegate body should consist of the members of the Standing Committee and delegates from the local churches. Heretofore, all who were present had the privileges of voting; and a question had to receive practically a unanimous vote to pass. This was now changed. All had the privilege of participating in the discussion, but if there were objections to the passage of a query, it could be passed by receiving the vote of two-thirds of the delegate body. It was further decided that no elder could serve on the Standing Committee more than two years out of four.

District meetings were approved of by Annual Meeting many years before they were definitely adopted in 1866. They were only to consider matters of local concern and were not permitted to publish a record of the meetings before 1876. In 1880 they were given the privilege of sending committees to settle trouble in local churches. This made it possible to relieve the General Conference of much of this unpleasant work.

## DIVORCE.

For fifty years no question has been up for consideration more often than the divorce. The church has always placed itself on record against the divorce evil; but there has not been a unanimity of sentiment as to whether a second marriage, while a former companion is living, is ever right. The difficulty comes from not being able to agree on the meaning of the Savior's words in Matt. 5:32; 19:9. So much dissatisfaction prevailed that in 1888 an extraordinary effort was begun to come to some definite conclusion. A committee was appointed consisting of John Wise, R. H. Miller, S. S. Mohler, Enoch Eby, and B. F. Moomaw. A year later S. H. Myers took the place of B. F. Moomaw. The committee entered into an exhaustive and earnest investigation of the subject. After two years of labor they failed to agree. At the Annual Meeting in 1890 a majority and a minority report were presented. R. H. Miller, S. S. Mohler and S. H. Myers presented the following: "We recommend Annual Meeting to decide that those who have never been taken into the chuch and taught the law of Christ shall be taken, where it is made clear that the divorce was for fornication. But after a person has once been taken into the church and taught the gospel doctrine on the subject of divorce, for the cause of fornication, they shall not be allowed to marry again."

John Wise and Enoch Eby presented a minority report to the effect that in no case should divorced persons be allowed to marry again, while the first partner was living, or be received into the church if they had two living companions. After a single speech on the majority report by R. H. Miller, and one on the minority report by John Wise, the matter was postponed for one year.

In 1891 both reports were thoroughly discussed and both were rejected by the meeting. Brother Robert's defense of his position was one of the strongest efforts that he ever made. The question was left as it had been until 1898, when a decision was passed that gave the right to receive into the church divorced persons if it could be clearly shown that the cause of separation was fornication. This answer has not given entire satisfaction, but it is probably as nearly right as any that we will get for some time.

### NONCONFORMITY.

On the question of nonconformity to the world Brother Robert always spoke with no uncertain sound. He believed pride to be one of the greatest enemies to the church. He believed that the Annual Meeting had a right to advise and pass judgment concerning the attire of the members. The church is a much safer guide to follow than the dictates of fashion. When the progressive element opposed decisions on this subject, he stood firmly against opening any gap for the worldly customs to enter the church.

He was interested, however, not simply in the external but also in the internal conditions. When the question came up at Hagerstown concerning the wearing of gold-framed spectacles, he was serving on the Standing Committee for the last time. He said to Brother D. L. Miller, who sat by his side, that it was useless to lop off a few branches here and there; better get at the root, and as the heart is the seat of pride, there is the place to work. He did not oppose a decision against worldlyism, but his mind was broad enough to see that after all men must be taught the principles of conformity to Christ and the church, if these principles are to be lived out in their lives.

### THE CHURCH NAME.

Brother Robert's last speech in Conference was against changing the name of the church. His main objection to change was that the brethren had not agreed on any name that would give more satisfaction than the old name, German Baptist Brethren. His position has proved to be right. Had the Conference adopted some of the names proposed, there would have been just as much dissatisfaction as ever. As it was, the old name was retained until 1907, when unexpectedly and almost unanimously, the name was changed to what appears to please all, " The Church of the Brethren." This was not, as many thought, a new name, for in some of the early publications the name was frequently applied to the church.

Brother Robert did not covet official standing at the Annual Meeting. He was moderator but once and reading clerk twice. He admitted that he was not the man for moderator because he had too many speeches to make. He preferred to be free from official duties. He was of greatest service in keeping order in the Conference by his ready grasp of the essential points and by his ability to make the matter clear to others.

He was an able man to help settle difficulties in the churches. Few men were sent oftener on these unpleasant tasks than he. He was nearly always foreman of the committee on which he acted. In some years much of his time was taken up in this work, going to as many as a dozen different places in all parts of the Brotherhood. In 1878 he and Brother Quinter were appointed to go to California to help settle difficulties there, but on account of his poor health they never went.

He experienced some trying ordeals. On one occasion, in Maryland, his committee was locked out of the meetinghouse by the elders to whose congregation he had been sent. Not to be outwitted, he at once announced the council for the grove near by. The council was held, with a large number present, and the mission successfully accomplished. He was once summoned to attend court at Dayton, Ohio. A case was being tried in which some of the Progressive Brethren were attempting to hold the church property, claiming that they were the original church. It was Brother Robert's task to prove to the court what the original church was. Though he had able lawyers opposing him, he easily held his own and received the decision of the court in his favor.

As foreman of committees he was very resourceful in meeting a trying situation. He could frequently suggest compromises by which all contending parties could be satisfied. He had the happy faculty of stating a proposition in such a way that it would give the least possible offense. An exciting or angry speech could never disturb his calm demeanor. His most effective means of handling a brother who was out of order was to let him make his speech, and then pass on as though the speech was merely a parenthetical expression.

## CHAPTER VIII.

### A Preacher of the Gospel.

Brother Robert was elected to the ministry by the unanimous vote of the church. Surely the choice was made by the direction of the Holy Spirit. He accepted the call with a deep appreciation of its sacredness and importance. Though at different times he was a farmer, debater, educator, author and editor, yet, he was above all other things, a preacher of the Gospel. Those who knew him most intimately probably remember most vividly his ministerial work.

He preached well from the first but he also gave evidence of continual growth. Those who heard him then testify to his power in the pulpit. After ten years' experience he visited Virginia, where he preached near the place of the Conference. Elder Daniel Hays, then a young man, gives us his impression of Brother Robert, in the following letter:

"It was in the year of 1869 that Annual Meeting was held near Salem, Va., and I had stopped at Bonsacks to attend the preaching service at this place during the week preceding Conference. While here Brother R. H. Miller preached one day in the forenoon. using as his text Acts 16:30: 'Sirs, what must I do to be saved?' It was easy to see that he was full of his subject, but he made no effort to impress this fact upon his audience by look or attitude either before or during the delivery of his sermon. He was perfectly natural. Well do I remember the glow of his expressive countenance, the twinkle of his eye and the steady flow of his thrilling words. He made no effort to shine by witty sayings, neither did he aim to clothe his strong points in striking colors; it was more like a refreshing downpour of rain upon the thirsty ground on a midsummer day. Then he had no distinguishing attitude nor gesture; it seemed rather a graceful and harmonious movement of his entire person in the delivery of his theme. Fully three-fourths of his sermon formed an introduction to the doctrine of his text. The self-sufficiency of the Bible as its own expositor was never more fully set forth. The Acts of the Apostles was shown to be in full accord with the teaching of our Lord as given in the Gospels. The brightest intellect could find matter too high for him to reach in the Sacred Scriptures while its saving truths came within the grasp of the simplest minds.

" Then from the *I* of the text and the *what do* of the text, he proceeded to its ultimate purpose, *to be saved,* and clinched the attention of his audience to a clearcut doctrinal statement drawn from the answer of Paul and Silas to the jailer's inquiry, ' Believe on the Lord Jesus Christ, and thou shalt be saved.' On the day of Pentecost when the Jews asked the apostles ' What shall we do?' Peter replied by saying. 'Repent and be baptized, every one of you in the name of Jesus Christ for the remission of sins, and ye shall receive the gift of the Holy Ghost.' These Jews were believers, but they were sinners and needed repentance and baptism for the remission of sins that they might receive the gift of the Holy Ghost. When Ananias came to Saul in Damascus, he did not tell him to *believe,* because he was a believer. Neither did he tell him to *repent* because he was a *penitent believer,* but he told him the next thing it was necessary for him to do: 'Arise and be baptized and wash away thy sins, calling on the name of the Lord.' But now when we come to the jailer at Philippi, a man who never heard the Gospel preached to him, and he asks the question, ' What must I do to be saved?' the apostle tells him to begin where *all must begin*: ' Believe on the Lord Jesus Christ and thou shalt be saved.'

" The beauty of his sermon was seen in the selection of his text and in the simplicity of its treatment. He did not confuse the minds of his hearers by giving them too much matter in detail. He reserved his strong points for the last, and gave them in the same strain with the same animation, without a hitch in voice or manner that would give the least occasion for a different opinion to arise in the mind, while deep down in the heart there was a conviction that this is all symmetrically true.

" At the home of Brother B. F. Moomaw, in the afternoon of the same day, Brother Miller appeared at the same advantage as a conversationalist, being equaled only by Brother Moomaw himself. I had heard ministers and other persons of distinction discourse on a variety of subjects before, but never did I hear a conversation so well poised, animated and sustained on social and religious topics as it came to me in the quiet of that southern home.

" Referring to his visit to the White House on the way, he introduced the brethren who were with him as Brother Metzger, of Illinois, Brother Jacob Miller, of Indiana, and so on, stating that they were on their way to Conference in Virginia and had stopped at Washington to pay their respects to the President of the United States. President Grant said in reply that it afforded him much pleasure to see his fellow-citizens from the West. He was glad to meet some of the good people of the West and he thanked them for the favor of giving him a call. Brother Miller remarked that he undertook the visit to the White House with the impression that it would be attended with some embarrassment, but he knew one thing, let it be as it would, he could at least *out-talk* the President."

A sermon that would so impress itself upon the minds of the hearers that they could vividly recall it after forty years must have been delivered with power. Those who have heard Brother Robert preach will at once recall his various characteristics mentioned by Bro. Hays. In the following advice, given to young preachers, Brother Robert speaks of qualities which seemed to him essential to the minister:

"The first and greatest thing to insure your success is the condition of your heart which is the center of preparation for the ministry as well as any other good work. There you must look for your spirit and power that makes your labor beneficial to the church. There you will feel that divine love to lead you to the object of man's salvation, warming up your own life to activity and zeal in the greatest cause for which man can labor.

"The next thing of importance is the improvement of your mind that you may be able to teach others.

Study one subject at a time. Do not scatter your mind over too much at once. Do not raise your expectation too high; you cannot expect to excel at first, but a continued effort will seldom fail. Do not get into the deepest doctrine or try to explain what you do not understand. Always quit when you get done, and be sure to get done before your audience gets tired.

"Never try to preach and act just like other men; be yourself; come out in your own strength; improve, convert and train your own nature to work in harmony and union with the Divine Spirit. If you are naturally inclined to be too mirthful, stop that at once; it will hurt your influence and injure your cause. If you are inclined to do doctrinal preaching, be careful not to become dry and tedious; you can only do good when there is life and spirit in your preaching, coming from the fountain of your heart. If you have the greatest ability, come down to the capacity of your audience; do not preach above them but to them as they are. Lead them up in knowledge and spirit to appreciate your labors and accept the truth. Make them love you by loving them.

"Never become a fighting preacher with hard words and soft arguments. Use kind words but make your arguments "hot and heavy." Let Jesus be the all-absorbing truth of your sermons to build up the sacred principles of life in your hearers. Never let yourself be the foremost thing you preach. A big 'I' spoils it all. If you have ability you need not tell it or show it in your actions. The people will find it out, probably all too soon; for then praises will injure you unless you have a good deal of Christ and common sense to keep you humble. If you have not great talent, you need all the more grace to bear you up when you see brethren hang their heads as though they were ashamed of your efforts. If you feel that you have failed, study, read and pray, and make every effort to succeed next time. If you have but one talent you will be the very preacher some will want to hear. No preacher pleases all persons or places; so do not think ill of those who may prefer to hear some one else beside yourself. Always quit before you tell all you know. Then you may be interesting every time you preach. Never waste time by making apologies and needless preliminaries."

One more extract from his pen will serve to show his love for the simplicity and charity of the fathers. Though he was a power in the pulpit, yet he never pretended to be more than an old-fashioned preacher.

### OLD-FASHIONED PREACHING.

"Once the preaching of the cross was done by men who talked of the spirit and power of preaching the Gospel, not of the style of the orator or his preaching. They preached to save the world and to make it better, to unite the church in love and kindness, in faith and practice, until its happiness, its peace and prosperity made it the happy home of God's children. All the churches look back to former days when old-fashioned men preached the Gospel 'without money and without price'; men who believed and toiled with their hands at home, journeyed on foot and on horseback over the mountains to preach the Gospel.

"The Methodist church can look back to the day when all over the land, in log houses and woods, their old-fashioned preachers in plain attire and humble manner preached the Gospel to the poor. Thousands were called into the church when it grew in strength and lived in peace and plainness. John Wesley ignored the gaudy fashion and pride of the world, but tried to save it by his old-fashioned preaching. Religion was then down where common men could work at it to save the people. Zeal and life and love seemed common to all. The old-fashioned preaching had in it the spirit of these old-fashioned men, and its power for good was felt wherever they went.

"So it has been with many denominations; they can now sing of the 'church's desolation.' The organ, the church festival, pride and style have carried them far away from the old-fashioned preachers, till none, save fine orators and beautiful speakers, must be called to please the ear; until rivalry in manners and style has more display than the meek and humble religion of Jesus. The great thing about these old-fashioned preachers was the spirit they had in them. They preached to build up the church and save sinners. They had self-denial and love for the cross of Christ, and love for all the saints, and love for all the world. They might have been mistaken in some things, but their mistakes were on the side of mercy and love, of self-sacrifice and forbearance. Our danger is of losing the spirit of these old-fashioned men, and letting the world give us its spirit and carry us away from the old landmarks, and set up contention and rivalry over things that destroy love and peace and bring no good to any one. Oh! let us keep the spirit of our fathers; let us work for that love and happiness that the church enjoyed in those days."

Brother Robert was a text preacher. He took a text and stayed with it. Again and again during a sermon would he come back and emphasize the words of his text. He did not digress far to bring in history, literature or ancedotes, but he did marshal a great many passages of Scripture to unfold and impress the meaning of his text. Other preachers were more brilliant in style and diction than he; but few men ever had more power of indelibly stamping the text and its meaning upon the minds of his hearers.

He was very careful in the preparation of his sermons. Even after he had reached the maturity of his strength, he was known to have spent weeks of study upon a text before attempting to use it. He seldom preached but that he was in full command of all his resources. If ever he became confused in the pulpit, he could readily trace the cause to a lack of careful preparation or to an over-abundance of self-confidence and too little reliance on the Holy Spirit. This, however, rarely happened, for humility and trust were two of his prominent characteristics.

His library was not extensive, about one hundred volumes in all. They are nearly all religious books and show that they were much used. Here is another evidence of the truth of the old warning:

"Beware of the man of few books." Among his books are Webster's Dictionary, Book of Common Prayer, several Greek-English lexicons, church histories, works on baptism, etc., Evidence of Christianity and Spurgeon's Sermons.

He had well-defined ideas on all important subjects and doctrines of the Bible. He was often appealed to by brethren who desired to be taught the doctrines of the Gospel more perfectly. Some of this correspondence appeared in the church publications to the edification of all the readers. He was appointed by Annual Meeting to assist Eld. L. W. Teeter in preparing comments on the New Testament. It was the desire and intention that his series of doctrinal sermons at Mt. Morris should be published. Had he lived to deliver them, this would, no doubt, have formed a valuable addition to our church literature.

His ministerial services were very extensive. For a third of a century he was continually active in his own and surrounding congregations. He had calls far and near to preach funerals. He was not a revivalist, but had few equals as a doctrinal preacher. In this way he was very useful to convince outsiders of the truth of the principles of the church, and thus prepare the way for the evangelist; or to indoctrinate those who had already been received and make them well established in the faith. His extensive work on committees gave him opportunities to preach all over the Brotherhood.

In the pulpit he manifested a marked individuality. One of his habits was to preach with one hand in his pocket. He did not rise and fall in gesticulative speech, but as Brother Hays put it, "There was a steady flow of thrilling words." There was dignity and sobriety in every action. His words were so simple that all could understand them and yet they possessed dignity and animation. There was a twinkle in the eye, a pleasant smile upon the countenance, and a kindness in every tone that exerted an inexplicable effect upon his hearers.

In the following chapter a few of his sermons are included. Some are published entire as he gave them; while others are synopses published in the church papers or taken from his own manuscript. Let the reader remember that while the words are here, the wonderful personality of the speaker is absent. You who have heard him can readily picture him as you read. You who have never heard him will be at a disadvantage; and be sure to keep this in mind before judging of the speaker's power from the printed sermons.

# CHAPTER IX.

## Selected Sermons.

### THE WAY.

"And an highway shall be there, and a way, and it shall be called the way of holiness; the unclean shall not pass over it; but it shall be for those: the wayfaring men, though fools, shall not err therein." Isaiah 35: 8.

The prophet has reference to the establishing of Christ's kingdom on earth. We want to come to our point and preach it to you so plain that you can all see it: A way is a road along which people can travel, can walk in it, no hinderance being there, nothing to turn them out of the path if they stay in it. And our text says it is plain enough, even for fools. Who are wayfaring men? They are those who travel, those who are going somewhere. But this way spoken of by the prophet is a plain way; can't well miss it if we try. The old prophet has told the truth in this matter. He has told us that it is so plain that none of us need stumble, none need fail, all can walk in that way. One says, "I cannot find this way. I have been looking for it for years and I cannot understand it." Ah, my friend, there is a veil over your eyes. You want to get that away and then you can see the way that is so plain. Yes, but you say, " I shall accept the Gospel and obey it "; another says " The Bible is not true. I look at you two and do not know what to believe." Stop, my friend, do not look at us; look to God, and see what he says; don't depend on what the preachers say.

Look at the infidel and ask him, "What am I going to receive by accepting your doctrine? What can you give that is better than what I now have?" Has he anything but woes to offer you? Do you gain anything by accepting his doctrine? Do you lose anything by refusing his doctrine? If you accept his teaching and live by it fifty years, will it do you any good?

But take the other side. Suppose you trample the Savior's precepts under foot, look at the awful doom. If you accept Christ's doctrine, see what you gain. If it is true you gain everything; if it is not, you lose nothing. You have all the good there is in the world if you accept "the way"; if it is not true you have lost nothing and are just as well off. The Word of God has lifted man from a slavish position, has put him upon the way of holiness, made him a useful member of society, and filled his heart with love and honor to God. If the infidel is right, we are happy if we reject his theory; if he is wrong we are happy anyway. You see "the way" is so plain that a fool cannot err therein. That is the difference between infidelity and Christianity.

"Well, you have not hit me, have not helped me, because I am not an infidel," says one. "Some men say that all men will be saved anyhow, and how shall I tell what is right? I am in doubt and trouble." Stop, kind sir, you have been trying to find a plain way in the dark. When Sawyer or Williamson comes up and tells you that all men will be saved whether they obey the Gospel or not, what will you gain if you follow them? If you believe their doctrine, will it benefit you? If they have told you the truth, what are you going to gain by it? If Williamson's theory be true can you lose anything by rejecting it? Has he anything to offer that will do you any good? Suppose you take his doctrine and it is false, has it made you wiser in any respect? But suppose you reject his doctrine, can you lose anything by it? Not a thing. If the Gospel be true, if the commands of God be true, look where you stand. You lose nothing by obeying or disobeying the Gospel, if Williamson's doctrine be true; but if it is not true, then you lose everything if you obey not the Gospel of the Lord Jesus Christ.

"But you still have not come to me," says another; "I am no infidel, no universalist, but I believe in the doctrine of election." Let us look at that doctrine a little. The scholars of Calvin tell us that we can be saved by election, can do nothing if we are not elected. We cannot work out our soul's salvation with fear and trembling as directed by Paul, but must stand here and wait to be either damned or saved. Calvin may elect you but God never did. Suppose you reject the commands of God, claiming to be one of the elect, are you not showing a bad light by staying back? Now if their theory be true, you can lose nothing by obeying the Gospel; but if it be not true, look where you stand. You lose heaven and eternal happiness. You are

God's if you obey, if you do not you lose all. Suppose you are a reprobate, and come to Jesus, obey him, follow him, can you lose anything? Come then as the publican; come as you are and be cleansed and become a child of God. Can you be led to ruin by coming to Jesus? Can you lose anything by accepting God's plain way? The way is clear and so plain that wayfaring men cannot err therein. The darkness does not come from the plain way. Then come, oh, come to this plain way of the Lord and be saved.

But here is another who says, "I am not troubled about election, or infidelity, or universalism, but that preacher over yonder says I can be saved without baptism." Now you are looking at the preachers again. Don't do that. He and I may stir up a terrible dust but that doesn't give you safe ground. You must look to Jesus who made this way plain, just so plain that even fools cannot err therein.

But let us look at this matter of baptism. We find it in the Book, and since it is in God's Book it is safe to look at it, safe to be baptized. If you can be safe without baptism, can you lose anything by being baptized? Have you gained anything by accepting the theory that you can be saved without baptism? Jesus was baptized in the Jordan, and will you not be safe in following him? Here you see it is safe to take the side of Jesus.

"Well, I feel all right," says some one about being baptized, "but smarter men than you say I can be saved by sprinkling and pouring." Stop, and don't look at the preachers; you are looking at the wrong place. Ask yourself the question: "What more can I gain by sprinkling or pouring than by baptism?" Suppose sprinkling and pouring water be true, what do you gain? Suppose they are not true, see what you lose. You may gain a little convenience, but you risk that without the authority of God. But look to Jesus! See him going down into the water and there being baptized. Look at the bowl of water and then at the river, and see which Jesus patronized, see which is the plain way, the safe way. I want you to see that the way is so plain that you cannot err therein. Philip and the Eunuch went down into the water, in the plain way, and obeyed the Lord there. Do not let some preacher lead you in this manner, but let some inspired man tell you how baptism was performed. You can lose nothing by doing as Jesus did. There are no doubts about that. All men are agreed that the man who goes down into the water and is baptized as Jesus was, is safe so far as his baptism is concerned. He can gain nothing by being sprinkled or poured with water; but he can gain all by being baptized. This is the plain way, the good old way wherein we shall walk and be safe.

But here comes still another man who says, "I believe just as you have stated it, all these things are plain to me, but I can be saved by being dipped once instead of three times as you teach." Oh, my friends, look to Jesus. He tells us how to be baptized; take his counsel, his mode and you lose nothing. He says, "Go teach all nations, baptizing them in the name of the Father and of the Son and of the

Holy Ghost." This is the plain way, God's way. This is the way to look at. The person dipped three times will pass for a baptized person in any part of Christendom; but not so with the person dipped but once. That way is not a plain way; there are doubts about it. It is with this like the other things we have been looking at, you can lose nothing by accepting the plain way.

But there is still another who says, "This learned man teaches that I can be saved without following Jesus in the matter of feet-washing." Oh, my friend, when will you quit looking at the preachers? Look to the Word of the Lord, it is a sure guide and always gives good definitions. Can the man who teaches you not to wash the feet of your brethren as Jesus did, promise you more than Jesus promised? Jesus says, "Happy are ye if ye do these things," and "if I your Lord and Master have washed your feet, ye also ought to wash one another's feet." This is the plain way, the way Jesus went, and you can lose nothing by going that way. You may lose much by going some other way; you may never find Jesus if you listen to the preacher, but you can find him if you take the plain way, the way of holiness. "No lion shall walk there; the redeemed shall walk there." Then come and walk in that way. Jesus stands ready to receive you and help you on that way. It is a safe way, for Jesus walked there. Time forbids my noticing many other things in that plain way. But let all of us try to get on that way and stay there, for it is the sure way, a tried way, a plain way and a way that leads right up to heaven.

## THE NEW COMMANDMENT.

"A new commandment I give unto you, that ye love one another as I have loved you." John 13: 34.

This commandment has reference to the righteousness of the saints in their fellowship one with another. It is of greatest importance because it is the divine, the heaven-born power to rule in all the church councils, assemblies of worship, and in Christian fellowship in the church militant. With this principle of love, all the business of church government turns on the oil of peace. All the worship and service of God is a sweetened cup of joy, and all the labor of the Christian is a yoke easy, a burden light.

Before this time Christ had taught the disciples to love God with all their hearts, to love their neighbor as themselves, and to love their enemies. But now he gives them a new command, to love one another as he had loved them. This shows that something more is taught than the love which the Jewish law required. It is a special love to govern, to rule in the heart of the Christians in all their relations to one another, as the family and household of God.

This makes it our duty to consider well, and maintain faithfully, the special love of this new commandment. It is the power, the bond of union, communion and fellowship among the saints. This sacred principle of love lies at the foundation of all our happiness; without it there is no real happiness for the people of God. Take the family to illustrate this truth: If the parents have no love for each other, the brothers and sisters no love for one another, all the wealth and honors of earth cannot bring happiness into such a family. So it is with the church; if love reigns not in it, happiness is not there.

It is required of us to accept the teachings of our Savior on this important doctrine of the Gospel, and realize in all its branches the sacred, saving power of love. First, to love God with all the heart. This shows how we must love God, because he first loved us and from this love all the blessings of time and eternity flow. All our enjoyments come from the great fountain of his love, which brings us under obligations to love him supremely. Our love to God is the true source of obedience. It is the power which makes all his service pleasant, and makes obedience to his commands the delight and joy of his people. By it they are made to love his Word, his works, his providence in all the mercies of man's redemption.

Second. We are to love our neighbor as ourselves. This some have rather skeptically said we cannot do. But a true understanding of the command will teach the blessing in it and the wisdom that appointed it for our good. It is the foundation of the "golden rule." It requires that we should so love our neighbor as to desire and labor that he should have and enjoy the same blessings that we, ourselves, possess. It does not require that we should destroy our own happiness for his benefit, nor that we should divide our property with him. But that we seek to give him any opportunity and means which we must depend upon for our own happiness.

This principle of love to our neighbor as ourselves would prevent us from doing anything to hinder, or destroy his happiness. It would destroy in us any desire to build up any party or order. That would give one man advantage over another. It is the broad principle of universal love, which seeks the good of all upon the truths, the laws of God and nature. It requires that we do good for our neighbor as we would have him do for us. This command does not set aside the other commands as we have referred to, but adds another more perfect branch to it. The disciples are commanded to love one another as Christ loved them. The apostle alludes to this when he says we shall do good unto all men, especially the household of faith, showing the fellowship of the saints to embrace a love more sacred than any other, save the supreme love of God.

First  We notice that this doctrine, that Christians shall love one another as Christ loved them, is the most perfect bond of union that can be made among the children of God. The love of Christ is strong and unchangeable: "Neither death, nor life, nor angels, nor principalities, nor powers, nor things present, nor things to come, nor height nor depth, nor any other creature shall be able to separate us from the love of God in Christ Jesus our Lord." This shows how strong and lasting is the love of Christ for his church. No power can break that bond of union; the apostles erred and failed in the weakness of their natures, but he has made the mercy seat a throne of grace, and his loving kindness changes not. Such love shed abroad in the heart is the bond of union among Christians, is the divine power God has given to make them one as the Savior prayed, "That they may be one as the Father and I are one."

Second. In this new commandment, Christ has revealed the wonders of forgiving love; when the disciples erred in judgment, word or action, his forgiving love healed the wound. Although they might so fail as to deny him, his forgiving love opens a way to a throne of grace, and is stronger than all their weakness. This forgiving love of our Savior is the model, rather the love itself, which should fill our own hearts with forgiveness for our brethren. The Savior would enforce this doctrine with a penalty, when he says: "If you forgive not one another their trespasses, your Father in heaven will not forgive you." How important then is this doctrine of forgiving love, when the want of it rejects us from a throne of grace. If God must forgive us all our sins, forgive us every day, surely we can forgive our brethren for all we have to bear with them. Forgiveness for our brethren requires only that we should sink deep in the new commandment, or rather it should sink deep into us.

This forgiving love implied in the new commandment, with all its sacred power, is much needed in our church councils, especially in troubles; with it there is a road, a way out of all our church difficulties; without it there is no remedy. There may be a form of words, a show of settlement, but without the Christlike, forgiving love in the heart, the formality is an empty shell, and worse, a feeling of bitterness, ready to break out when another stroke of Satan comes. Nothing but the love of the new command, pure, Christlike, forgiving love, can sweeten the bitter cup. We should drink of that love until it be shed abroad and deep in our hearts, to qualify us for the work of faith and the labor of love in the church.

This forgiving love of Jesus runs out to meet and restore the erring brother, like the prodigal's father; while yet afar off, his father runs to meet him; kills the fatted calf for him, puts the best robe on him, calls a feast because his heart is full of forgiving love and full of happiness. But the unforgiving, elder brother fills his own bitter cup. He stands without because there is no joy for him where the feast of forgiving love rejoices over the prodigal's return. Forgiving love is the great peacemaker which reconciles the children of men to one another and to God.

Third. We shall love our enemies. In this command much of the Christian spirit is required. This spirit was in our Savior when "He gave himself for the just and the unjust," and when he prayed for those who crucified him: "Father, forgive them for they know not what they do." Out of the principle of this command comes the truth that we return good for evil, and pray for those who despitefully use us.

This heaven-born love, that seeks the good of our neighbor, is the principle on which a sinner is saved.

While we were enemies Christ died for us. It is the love of God reaching fallen, rebellious man that saves him; and this command to love our enemies truly would make the disciple like his Father in heaven, who sends his rain on the just and on the unjust.

In this age of elastic sentiment, some have contended that they could love their enemies and go to war with them, using all the means in their power to destroy them; but surely this cannot be a scriptural view of love. Had Christ loved the world in such a manner, no sinner could find redemption in the wounds of our Savior. But his love for the enemies of truth, offers them pardon and mercy on the peaceable terms of the Gospel.

This doctrine that we should love our enemies, puts into our hands the most powerful weapons of victory. By love an enemy may be conquered and made a friend. By force he may be subdued and made a slave. The victory gained by love is complete, even over an enemy. It is God's way, his means of converting sinners, and he has committed it unto us, that we may, by it, work for the victory of the cause of Christ.

We now come to consider the new commandment as something more, in the doctrine of love, than has before been taught among the children of men.

Third. This new commandment has in it the doctrine of self-denial. It shows how, like Christ, we should labor for the good of the church. "Though he was rich, for our sake he became poor, that we, through his poverty, might be made rich." He humbled himself and in due time he was exalted. This shows his great desire for the church to be exalted and what he did to confer honor, and glory and greatness upon it.

We should so love the church as to humble ourselves to it in our opinions and our views; in all our ways we should be submissive to our brethren. This qualifies us to exalt and honor the church in all her councils and decisions. Because we love the brethren, we respect and submit to their counsel in Annual Meeting, and labor in our weakness to build up and honor the church above our own opinions and all the institutions of men. This love for the brethren makes it a pleasure to accept their counsel in dress and nonconformity to the world. It makes us feel that their counsel is the most safe and sure way for us to take in all matters where there is no "thus sayeth the Lord." This love which makes us humble and self-denying among our brethren, and at the same time greatly respect their councils, it is the sure road, the safe way to peace and happiness in the church for which Christ died.

Fourth. The appointed means of the Gospel is a divine faith and practice, the channels of love God has opened for the fellowship of his children. It is through these channels of divine truth that we should love one another "as Christ loved us." As the love of Christ embraced all truth of revelation, all the righteousness and obedience of the Gospel on the one hand, and his church on the other, and for salvation brought them together, so the love of Christianity embraces one another in gospel truth, righteousness and obedience. As the love of Christ for the saints has given them all blessings of gospel light and opened the eyes of their understanding, giving knowledge of spiritual life by a change of heart, so through every blessing and mercy they receive must and does flow the stream of brotherly love to all the kindred spirits of Christ, making a more perfect and sacred union under the second covenant than that made by the first.

Fifth. This love of Christ was spiritual in its work, design and blessing. It was manifested to a spiritual people, those who were born of the Spirit and adopted into a spiritual kingdom. His instruction to them was on spiritual subjects; his conversation was about spiritual things, to turn their minds to the righteousness brought from heaven. He chose them out of the world to sanctify unto himself a peculiar people, zealous of good works, and he continued with them a constant Companion and faithful Friend. Such should be our love for the brethren; we should choose them as our company, associate with them as those who feared the Lord and spake often one to another. Our conversation should be like his, about spiritual things, to give instruction and encouragement.

Sixth. The love of Christ to the church is shown in his labor and work to teach and qualify the disciples for the great mission of love, to call sinners to repentance. He would teach them how to preach and pray and labor for the spread of the Gospel, that others might hear the truth and believe. So ought the brethren to love one another in that manner which favors a union, working together like the man Christ Jesus for the salvation of sinners, to call them unto the faith and practice of the primitive church; for unto that they are called by the Savior and his apostles. And for them, for the church, and for the saving truths of the Gospel, we should be led to labor as *brethren at work* for the spread of primitive Christianity.

We have tried to set forth some of the blessings derived from love, as the bond of union and fellowship among Christians, and now, to cover our failures, we pray God to help us to realize the commandment of our Savior when he says: "A new commandment I give unto you; that ye love one another as I have loved you."

### SAVED BY THE POWER.

"Who are kept by the power of God through faith unto salvation ready to be revealed in the last time." 1 Peter 1: 5.

All the hope and trust of the Christian are founded on the power of God in salvation. Man, who has not the wisdom or power to save himself, must look beyond the finite, beyond the feeble arm of creature agency up to the infinite power and wisdom of Jehovah, to find safety and certainty in redemption. Salvation, founded upon the work of divine power, in the whole life of the Christian, in his faith, in his practice, in his experience, is the surety of his victory and triumph at last, as it is of his peace and happiness at present.

Some persons readily admit the power of God in

creation, but deny his power in the laws of nature, attributing the works of nature to nature's laws. Such are properly termed scientists, who decide that laws in nature govern all things and contend that by living in obedience to the laws of nature, man reaches the highest state of happiness possible for him to attain. But from the laws of nature come famine, pestilence and death as well as prosperity and life; thus making the laws of nature the greatest source of misery and death, and he who trusts in them for hope of salvation must be confounded when he sees that all nature, as well as himself, is doomed to die.

Others admit the power of God to save man through his miracles, but deny his power to work out man's salvation through the laws of nature and revelation, thus denying all the power of God to save man through means, and making the laws and commands of God in revelation of no effect or force in salvation. This theory takes a part of the truth only because it limits the power of God in salvation to miracles alone.

In the divine government of God, he no more works without the laws of nature and revelation than he does without miracles; and to set aside either of them in God's providence and plan of redemption is a dangerous error opposed to the truths of the Bible. In leading the children of Israel out of Egypt, God did it by his divine power, but it was done through the laws of revelation and of nature as well as by miracles. He gave his command to Moses and Israel; this was his law revealed to them. The children of Israel journeyed from Rameses to Succoth. When they came to the Red Sea God "caused the sea to go back by an east wind." Here is a miracle through the laws of nature. God delivered the children of Israel out of Egypt by his divine power, and he did it through miracles, through his commands and laws revealed to them in such a plain manner that it cannot be denied.

Those who found revelation on miracles alone do so because they think if the works of man have anything to do with it, salvation would not be of God. But this is an erroneous view, because God can work by his power through human agency as well as through miracle; in fact, all of his providence and redemption as revealed in the Bible is through human agency. God's salvation to the human family was through Noah; his miracles to the children of Israel through Moses, and the agency of the prophets and lawgivers; and when we come to the Gospel, salvation is there given to man by the power of God through human agency as well as through miracles.

This brings us to see the strong ground on which the Christian stands. Accepting the whole truth of revelation he looks to the power of God to save him. When the seasons roll around and the rains come and bring a plentiful harvest, he remembers that it is "Our Father" in heaven who sends the rain on the just and the unjust. He looks beyond the laws of nature up to the divine power from which all his blessings come. So in all the plan of salvation, he accepts the laws, the commands of God, knowing that they were given by the divine power; and he obeys them, feeling that they are so many ways and means through which the divine power keeps and saves him.

In this manner all the works of nature, all the laws and commands of God are a continual source of peace to the Christian. They all come freighted with blessings to feed the wants of his soul, body and spirit; they are the means appointed of God to save him. They may bring old age, they may bring affliction and trouble, they may bring pestilence and want, but then we know that there is a power working over all to make every providence, every pain and sorrow a means through which the divine power is preparing us for mansions of bliss.

The divine power can bring the right blessing out of a Joseph sold into slavery; can turn all the sorrows of Jacob into fullness of joy; can make deliverance to Israel sweeter on account of a bondage in Egypt; can heal the afflictions of Job and make him know that his "Redeemer liveth."

Another thing connected with the power of God is his decrees and purposes. The salvation of man was foreordained, and all the means by which the plan of redemption is made perfect were foreordained. When God purposed and decreed the salvation of man, he foreordained the plan. The law of faith and obedience to all the commands and precepts were decreed and given by the divine power. As the apostle says, "You are created in Christ Jesus unto good works, which God has before ordained that ye should walk in them." Every command is made efficient in the divine purpose and decreed as a means through which the divine power keeps and saves the heirs of salvation. How dangerous and rebellious to set aside the commands or any part of the plan of salvation which God has foreordained. Or who has a right to change the ordinances that God has given to the church by his Son?

To get the truth on the subject of how we are saved by the power of God, let us go back to the apostles' day when our text was written. There was a people kept by the power of God in that age. and the way it was done is the important truth we wish to learn. And we are thankful that God has told us in the Gospel how he kept the church in that day. They were led by inspired teachers along the pathway that leads from earth to heaven. In this pathway are baptism, the Lord's supper, the communion, the holy kiss and all the rest of God's commands which he foreordained that they should walk in them. The church then was safe, and the gates of hell could not prevail against it, because God kept it in his own way, and the people whom God keeps are eternally safe.

As Noah was safe, kept by the power of God in his own appointed way while a sinful and rebellious world sank to rise no more, so in the day of judgment, will the primitive Christian be safe, who has been kept in God's own way, while a sinful and rebellious world is driven from the presence of God and the glory of his power. What a contrast between the two companies who stand before God awaiting his judgment. On the one side are those who are kept by his power, in his own way. In that company are those who have continually walked in all the commands of the Lord blameless, have kept the faith once delivered to the saints, and in a meek and quiet spirit have followed the good works which were foreordained and given of God.

But where stand the other company of those who have wilfully neglected God's commands, who have refused to obey from the heart that form of doctrine once delivered to the saints? See them adorning themselves with gold, pearls and costly array and in all the fashions of the world. See what a vast company has departed from the simplicity of the truth as it is in Christ Jesus, from the commands by which God kept and saved the primitive church.

When you have looked at these two companies, dear hearer, turn and look at yourself. Are you kept by the power of God in the same way the primitive Christians walked? Are you kept in love with the church and all the laws and commands God has given it? Are your soul, body and spirit adorned with all the meekness, the grace and obedience to good works which God has before ordained that you should walk in them? Look to your own heart and see if he is keeping you in his own way that you may be saved by the power of God.

## TRUE GLORY.

(Baccalaureate sermon delivered at Ashland College, June 19, 1881.)

"Thus saith the Lord, let not the wise man glory in his wisdom, neither let the mighty man glory in his might, let not the rich man glory in his riches. But let him that glorieth glory in this, that he understandeth and knoweth me, that I am the Lord which exercise loving kindness, judgment and righteousness in the earth: for in these things I delight, saith the Lord." Jer. 9: 23, 24.

In delivering this farewell sermon to you, the members of this graduating class, it is both natural and reasonable that we should invoke the blessings of God to attend you through your future life, and point you to his truth as the last lesson given you within the walls of this college. Since your collegiate course is complete, and you are about to go out into the world to play your part in the great drama of life, it is fitting that our deep concern for your welfare should mainly rely on the truths of Christianity, which have governed us in your literary training, and which we hope will govern you in your future life.

There are now, have ever been, and ever will be men who govern and rule in the world by means of power and influence that they possess. From the highest ranks of society down to the lowest, in religion, politics, and social life, some men are ruling spirits, moulding the character of the social and business world and directing it to its weal or woe. In this class of men we have our greatest interest. To them the world must look. And for their advantages they owe to God a great account. Somewhere in these ranks of men we expect you, my young friends, soon to take a place. For these reasons we adopt this text for this occasion, that its truth may have some weight to determine the future character and work of those who have enjoyed the labors and care of this college, to prepare them for usefulness in the world.

"Let not the wise man glory in his wisdom." The first thought in our text is a warning of danger to you in your future pathway of duty. All the human wisdom you may have obtained, and however great your attainments may be, without the truth of Christianity to inspire your future with sacred and Godlike affection for the good of mankind, will be in vain and possibly lost. You should not glory in your attainments but in the "wisdom which is from above." Let your attainments serve you as a means of doing good in the world and make that purpose the great object of your life. Let your purpose be higher than any selfish object and let the glory of your character brighten the great mission of man in the world, to glorify God. This text will teach you not to let your learning exalt you. The young man beginning life smoothly and with bright prospects before him needs the warning in our text not "to glory in his wisdom," but let a higher view of your attainments rather teach you humility. As you go from this college building, bidding us farewell, let the power and influence of your learning be directed by the higher view, which will turn your labors through this life into the pathway which leads to the reward in the life to come.

"Neither let the mighty man glory in his might." Another warning to you. Men of power seem to forget the wants of others, lose their sympathy and are often found ruling over their inferiors with tyranny. You go out from here with advantages and power in some respects above the mass of mankind. But let not your advantages make you look down on others. Take your stand in the common walks of life with the people, and let your life be a means to elevate theirs. Let your learning improve theirs. Impart to the world some benefits from your own education, and most of all let the sacred truths of Christianity make you glory in the might of him whose blessings have made you what you are, and given you such opportunities to reach all that a well-spent life can ever enjoy. This text condemns every form of tyranny and oppression. The strong should not oppress the weak. It is God's plea for the poor and helpless. And from it we hope you may learn to use the power you have attained to defend the rights, and turn the blessings of life into the humble pathway of the poor and helpless. Education has always been the enemy of tyrants, while it has plead the cause of the poor. With the mass of the people well educated, the mighty man loses his power to oppress them, and in it the rights of the weak find the strongest protection.

"Let not the rich man glory in his riches." You may at first view conclude this part of our text does not apply to you, because you have not the riches alluded to. But as it is true that riches are a power in this world, which often oppresses the poor, so it is true that education is the only power to defend them against the encroachment. Learning is a power, it is true, but less than any other power is it inclined to oppress the weak, and more than any other is it able to stand against the strong. This part of our text also teaches us the vanity of trusting in riches; that earthly things alone cannot satisfy the wants of the immortal spirit; that all there is of human wisdom, might and wealth cannot give happiness to the immortal mind unless the truth of revelation brings them in harmony with the divine will. You may have them all combined, but if not controlled by the Gospel of Christ in its sacred truth, you may be a curse to the world, and blast the image of God in your own immortal nature, till it would be better for the world if you had not lived in it, and better far if you had not been born.

"But let him that glorieth, glory in this that he understandeth and knoweth me." This part of our text opens the glory there is for you to understand and know God with all your knowledge. If this be lacking, life is a failure. To understand and know God is the brightest glory of man. This divine radiance, which is the light of the world, is made doubly strong by being blended with the advantages you have and the attainments you have made. This is the highest and greatest knowledge ever attained by man. With it your education is riches far more than pearls or diamonds, because by it the mind and heart are adorned with the richer pearl of great price. The young man who starts out in life to meet its battles without the wisdom of God to direct his course, meets its dangers all in doubt, and in its trial he is an easy prey to every vice. But the young man whose heart is fixed on the Rock of Ages, whose mind is stored with wisdom from above, is worthy and deserves the confidence of all. And if you hold fast to the religious and moral training you have received here, there is no danger for your safety and no doubt for your success in life.

Your education has been the study of God in nature, in science. Every truth you have learned is that much knowledge of the law and mind of God. To know and understand him in nature's great book insures your usefulness in the path of duty by bringing you nearer to him. Every truth in nature carries you back to its fountain where you may know and understand more of God. You need, too, to know him in his revealed truth in Christ with all the perfection of wisdom manifested for you. To know him is the riches of understanding which turns all knowledge to the glory of God and man.

"I am the Lord which exercise loving kindness, judgment and righteousness in the earth." With you there has been much pains taken, time and money spent, to cultivate and improve all your powers. Paul-like you have been brought up at the feet of Gamaliel; your advantages increase your obligations to God and the world. To exercise loving kindness, judgment and righteousness is the solid foundation God would make for your character. On this foundation you can stand against all opposition. Kindness to all you meet in life; it costs but little and pays much. It will smooth your own pathway and bless and win the world around you. It will give a thousand little helps to others and bring as many back to you. We earnestly hope you will not make your way through life without kindness to all.

"Judgment." This text means to deal justly with all men, to do right in regarding the wants and conditions of other men. This will give you business, give you opportunity to do good in the world. More, it will make you strong to plead the cause of the poor, and defend the rights of the weak. Let the divine law make up your judgment in all cases, and mercy be mingled with its execution, then your life will be a blessing to you and to the world in which you live.

"Righteousness." This last item in our text is full of importance to you. Because of your superior learning young men like you, adorned with righteousness of Christ, are the brightest hopes of the world, the highest joy of parents, the greatest happiness to others. We pray that righteousness may be a radiance round your pathway of duty down the stream of life, until its evening sun has set, and prepared you for the reward of a well-spent life.

We bid you farewell, praying God's blessing may ever attend you, and save you at last.

## THE CHRISTIAN'S WARFARE ENDED.

(Funeral sermon of John Studebaker, the father of the famous Studebaker Bros., at South Bend, Ind., Dec. 17, 1877.)

"I have fought a good fight, I have finished my course, I have kept the faith. Henceforth there is laid up for me a crown of righteousness, which the Lord, the righteous judge, shall give me at that day: and not for me only, but unto all them also that love his appearing." 2 Tim. 4: 7-8.

The language of the text gives the impressive figure of an old soldier when his warfare is ended, passing from labor to reward. It is his last look back over the many hard fought battles of his life. He says first, "I have fought a good fight." This language expresses the feeling of the apostle, when he contemplates the life of the Christian with its trials and labors as a warfare ended, the victory won, and the old soldier lays his armor by. The soldier's life is full of interest, trials and dangers. Though the battle is long and hard, the fight is a good one, because it brings the victory at last. How well this thought in the text applies to Father Studebaker; he could look back over a long life full of trials, misfortunes and sufferings, but victory and deliverance have come. His last battle is over. His passport is sealed to go home. But ere he starts, he selects this text to tell us that the fight with all of its troubles has been a good one.

Another thought making this text impressive is the warfare; it is not alone for the benefit of self. Thousands reap the reward of the soldier's suffering and victories. Many rejoice in peace and prosperity where the soldier bled and died for the cause of others. So the apostle in many hard fights suffered long. And how many are richly blessed by the labors of that soldier of the cross! So too, our old father, a faithful soldier in his integrity, fought battles of life for the good of others, teaching and defending the sacred principles of his religion, in industry and honesty, thus laying the foundation of prosperity for the family who in business and influence are equal to any in the West. They, today, should look back to the life of their father and feel the truth of the text, that he has fought a good fight for them. This thought, too, sweetens the bitterest cup in the life of a soldier, to see that his suffering is the coffer in which the richest jewels are kept. In the land of contest and trial, the golden sheaves are gathered for the angel harvest.

Second. The apostle says, "I have finished my course." In this are expressed the feelings of one who has laid down the cross and is ready, waiting to receive the crown. The work is finished; then comes the change from labor to reward. Oh, how sweet is rest to the worn-out and afflicted soldier, when he receives his long furlough to go home; his final discharge signed; his passport sealed! He gladly sings,

> "When I can lay my armor by,
> And dwell with Christ at home."

The Christian sees much of God in the work when it is furnished. Trials, afflictions and sorrows may have made up his days and years, but God appointed them all and his divine power safely keeps his faithful soldier when the storms of sorrow rage. The work is finished, but how good it is for the soldier who can stay till his work is well done. He takes his passport and goes home but he leaves the work he has finished, a blessing to all behind him. The apostle has gone home, but what a glory in the work he has left us! So it is with our father; his place in the family circle is vacant but his Christian example still lives in the hearts of his friends, —a treasure richer than jewels and more lasting and bright than marble glass.

Third. "I have kept the faith." Paul looks over his past life, and speaks of the great joy and comfort in his faith unshaken, unwavering, when he comes to cross the river. Through all the misfortunes of life, in perils by land and sea, in prison, and among false brethren, in the cold, damp dungeon at Philippi, his feet made fast in the stocks, his faith could find songs of redeeming love to sing at midnight, the prison was cheered with the hope of immortal life and the crown of righteousness soon to be given. His faith in God he kept to the last, even when led to the block of Nero and all men had forsaken him. "Nevertheless," said he, "the Lord stood by me and strengthened me."

"Henceforth there is a crown of righteousness which the Lord, the righteous judge, shall give me at that day." A crown implies all of the honor and power and wealth that can be conferred upon the conqueror when the warfare is ended. Thus Paul represents the glory of eternal life given to the soldier of the cross when the victory is won. By "henceforth," Paul means that the crown is now ready, waiting for me. Not a crown of gold, pearls and diamonds to give earthly honor and power, but a crown of righteousness to give the heir of God; "an inheritance incorruptible, undefiled, that fadeth not away, and reserved in heaven." Our old father would have this text at his funeral, because it points his children to his hope in the crown of righteousness, richer than all earthly things and waiting for him beyond the river. "The Lord the righteous judge shall give" that crown when the soldier gets his last discharge and comes home. It is not a bounty of a few acres of land or a few dollars of money, but a right to sit with him on his throne, to be kings and priests in the resurrection, made in the glorious likeness of the Son of God, crowned to reign with him forever.

This crown the Lord will give at that day, a time appointed when the Judge shall give the crown. We may all soon change worlds and go to take that crown when the Judge says, "Come, ye blessed of my Father, inherit the kingdom." As Abraham looked for a city whose builder and maker is God, so our old father did. Out of his long afflictions on earth, he could look beyond to that city where no sickness, sorrow, pain nor death ever enter its jasper walls, no funeral trains ever walk its golden streets.

"And not to me only but to all them that love his appearing." This shows the ardent desire of the apostle for the welfare of others. Still like the faithful soldier, his warfare is not for himself only but also for the good of others. This great government is the fruit of the revolutionary struggle that our fathers made. The soldier there fought and bled for our good as well as his own. This point in the text we can realize when we think how great are the blessings given to the church by the labors of the apostle. What a heritage for after-generations has been given by the labors of the old apostle, to lead them on to righteousness and to victory. How truly this beautiful thought in the text, "Not for me only," applies to Father Studebaker. Few men could be found who had more concern for the welfare of others than he. His charities were often more than his circumstances would allow. His family, the church and the poor were these objects in the work of his busy life. And we are glad to see that after so much labor and love in his eventful life, plenty and peace crowned his old age. This text points his children back to all the labors of his life, with the thought, "Not for me only," and then points us forward to the crown of glory with the same words, "Not for me only."

To our old mother, who has been bereaved of her husband, we can give no earthly comfort sufficient to fill the heart left aching by death. In your declining years, your pathway will be lonely even amidst all the comforts earth can give. But you can turn from the sorrows of earth, where death is written upon all, to the brightest hopes of eternal life, and from the grave of the risen Savior, learn the glories of the resurrection in the likeness of God. Go to the throne of grace and there wait all the days of your appointed time till your change comes. Trust in God for support and help when all the powers of earth have failed, for he is able to make "all things work together for good to them that trust him."

And to you children, it seems needless that we should tell you how great is your duty to your weeping mother, for you, whose tenderness has never failed in all the long affliction of your father, cannot fail to appreciate the duty you owe to a good mother when affliction, old age and weakness have come upon her. All her enjoyment in this life is shallow in the cup and must be filled with the love and kindness of her children. We would not tell you not to weep, but rather thank God that children have tears to shed when bidding farewell to one who has done so much for them. But we pray that you will long treasure in your hearts the bright example death cannot destroy, and may it turn your hearts more to the spirit world when you go to the grave to weep. And keep in view the empty tomb of a risen Savior to cheer the darkness of death with the glories of a resurrection, when this corruption shall have put on incorruption, and this mortal shall have put on immortality, and all the sorrows of death are swallowed up in eternal life. May God bless you all.

## PROPHETICAL EVIDENCE OF CHRISTIANITY.

(Delivered at Mount Morris, Illinois, January 9, 1892.)

"We have also a more sure word of prophecy; whereunto ye do well that ye take heed, as unto a light that shineth in a dark place, until the day dawn, and the day star arise in your hearts." 2 Peter 1: 19.

The evidence of Christianity, derived from prophecy, is one of the strongest that can be brought forward. It is God leaving witness to the children of men that the book of revelation is founded on divine authority. This, with the miracles of the Bible, constitutes one kind of evidence that we may call external, because it is a witness to sustain the doctrine and truth of the Bible. There is another class of evidence in the Bible, to which we will allude in our next discourse.

It requires as much wisdom and power to foretell and fulfill the prophetic declarations of the Scriptures as it does to perform their miracles, and the testimony is positive when clearly established. The evidence from prophecy is made clear when the circumstances and events foretold are such that no human knowledge could have foretold them. Especially, when such prophecy relates to important events containing a number of great men, cities and nations, extending through a long period of time; and when such prophecies are fulfilled in such clear and plain manner that there can be no reasonable doubt of the literal fulfillment, the divine power and wisdom is clearly proven.

This evidence drawn from prophecy is made the test of truth against all idolatry in the forty-first chapter of Isaiah: "Produce your cause, saith the Lord; bring forth your strong reasons, saith the King of Jacob. Let them bring them forth, and show us what will happen: let them show the former things, what they be, that we may consider them, and know the latter end of them; or declare us things for to come. Shew us the things that are to come hereafter, that we may know that ye are gods: yea, do good, or do evil, that we may be dismayed, and behold it together." Here power to foretell future events that are beyond human wisdom or reason to know, is admitted to be positive evidence of divine power and wisdom.

God sets this evidence before Israel in Isaiah 48: 5: "I have even from the beginning declared it to thee, before it came to pass I showed it thee; lest thou should say, Mine idol hath done them." These future events are foretold for the special purpose of proving that there is a God who controls all things after the councils of his own will.

We will examine this testimony by referring to some of the greatest men, cities, and nations of which the prophets speak: Babylon, the capital of Chaldea, contained, according to classic history, not less than one hundred square miles. Both Isaiah and Jeremiah give many particular circumstances concerning its destruction, nearly one hundred years before it was destroyed. Isaiah 13: 19-22: "And Babylon, the glory of the kingdoms, the beauty of the Chaldees' excellency, shall be as when

God overthrew Sodom and Gomorrah. It shall never be inhabited, neither shall it be dwelt in from generation to generation; neither shall the Arabian pitch his tent there; neither shall the shepherds make their fold there. But wild beasts of the desert shall lie there; and their houses shall be full of doleful creatures; and owls shall dwell there, and satyrs shall dance there. And the wild beasts of the islands shall cry in their desolate houses, and dragons in their pleasant palaces: and her time is near to come, and her days shall not be prolonged."

Isaiah 21: 2 also foretells that Babylon shall be destroyed by the Medes. Jeremiah 51: 11 foretells the same things concerning the utter destruction of that great city. First, that the city and its walls shall be utterly thrown down and destroyed: Second, that it shall never be inhabited, and no man shall dwell there from generation to generation; that the Arab shall not pitch his tent there, neither shall the shepherd make his sheepfold there, but the wild beasts shall dwell in their houses and in their pleasant palaces. This prophecy concerning Babylon has been fulfilled so clearly that for many generations the ruins of the great city have been a lonely, desolate habitation for wild beasts, wholly deserted by man as though they were the haunted grave of the Chaldees' greatness.

The third point in this prophecy is that Babylon should be dstroyed by the Medes and the Persians. This prophecy, made by Isaiah, one hundred and seventy years before it was destroyed, is fulfilled to the very letter, and cannot fail to be clear evidence of the inspiration of the Bible. And further, as intimated in Isaiah 13: 19, and Jeremiah 51: 39, Babylon should be surprised and suddenly destroyed; so we learn from history that in a great festival of Babylon, Cyrus entered the city by the channel of the river and took the city by surprise.

Nineveh, another city of ancient times, of equal if not greater size than Babylon, is another test of prophecy. Jonah was sent to warn the city of its impending doom. He speaks of its size in the third chapter and third verse; he says Nineveh was an exceeding great city of three days' journey. Classic history puts it at sixty miles in circumference. Nahum 3: 13: "Behold, thy people in the midst of thee are women: the gates of thy land shall be set wide open unto thine enemies: the fire shall devour thy bars." Verse fifteen: "There shall the fire devour thee: the sword shall cut thee off, and it shall eat thee like the canker worm." Verse nineteen: "There is no healing thy bruise, thy wound is grievous."

In Nahum 2: 9, 10, we hear it is to be raked of its treasures, its silver and gold. Zephaniah 2: 13, 14, tells us that Nineveh shall be desolate and dry like a wilderness, but flocks shall lie there. Not like Babylon, never to be inhabited by man, but never to be rebuilt.

Mr. Layard, in excavating some of the ruins of Nineveh, found, as the prophet Nahum had said, that it had been burned with fire, as proven by the charred remains still standing. Also Mr. Layard could not find any treasures or images of value in all the ruins he excavated, thus showing the truth of the prophecy in all these particulars. And further in excavating Nineveh, on some of the alabaster slabs are found the names of the Jewish kings and the Assyrian kings found in the Bible; thus proving the truth of Jewish history as well as prophecy.

Egypt is so prominent in the Scriptures and in history that we would expect to find the truth of the Bible and the authenticity of the Scriptures tested by prophecies concerning the future destiny of Egypt. The prophecies concerning it are very clear. Ezekiel 30: 25, 26: "I will strengthen the arms of the king of Babylon, and the arms of Pharaoh shall fall down; and they shall know that I am the Lord, when I shall put my sword in the hand of the king of Babylon, and he shall stretch it out upon the land of Egypt. And I will scatter the Egyptians among the nations, and disperse them among the countries; and they shall know that I am the Lord." Ezekiel 29: 19: "Therefore thus saith the Lord God; Behold, I will give the land of Egypt unto Nebuchadrezzar, king of Babylon; and he shall take her multitude, and take her spoil, and take her prey; and it shall be the wages for his army."

Here it is foretold that Nebuchadrezzar, king of Babylon, should conquer Egypt and scatter the Egyptians among all nations and countries; and classic history teaches us that it was literally fulfilled. Ezekiel 30: 13: "And there shall be no more a prince in the land of Egypt." We know that the line of the Pharaohs has been destroyed and there has not been, and is not now, a prince of the land of Egypt to rule her people, but foreign powers rule a feeble country that was once the most powerful nation in the East. Even this is as Ezekiel said it should be. Ezekiel 29: 15: "It shall be the basest of kingdoms; neither shall it exalt itself any more above the nations."

Here is a plain prophecy fulfilled before the eyes of the world for more than eighteen hundred years, making strong and undeniable evidences of the authenticity of the Scriptures. The future destiny and final destruction of the great nations and cities, foretold by the prophets and fulfilled as they are before the eyes of the world, is conclusive evidence of the authenticity of the Bible.

But there are prophecies concerning the Israelites which are, if possible, stronger proof that the Bible is an inspired book. Moses in the book of Deuteronomy, 31: 29, says to the Israelites, "For I know that after my death ye will utterly corrupt yourselves, and turn aside from the way which I have commanded you; and evil will befall you in the latter days; because ye will do evil in the sight of the Lord, to provoke him to anger through the work of your hands."

Moses speaks in particular concerning the punishment of Israel in Deut. 28: 64: "And the Lord shall scatter thee among all people, from one end of the earth even unto the other; and there thou shalt serve other gods, which neither thou nor thy fathers have known, even wood and stone." Here is a prophecy of Moses, that Israel should be dispersed among all nations, made fifteen hundreds years before it was fulfilled. And we know that it is so plainly brought to pass in all its particulars that no skeptic can doubt, for no human wisdom could foresee such an unnatural event as scattering one people among all the nations of the earth. This same prophecy was repeated by the Savior nearly fifteen hundred years after it was delivered by Moses, with the addition that Jerusalem should be trodden under foot of the Gentiles until the time of the Gentiles be fulfilled. Luke 21: 24.

Although Israel is scattered among all nations, they still remain God's peculiar people, a separate race from all the nations of the earth. This is an unnatural exception that the Jews should dwell among all nations and never become amalgamated with them by intermarriage. Since they have remained a separate people and a distinct race according to prophecy, we are left with no reasonable doubt that a divine Providence rules over this people, to carry out a greater prophecy that they will be gathered into their own land. Ezekiel 11: 16, 17: "Thus saith the Lord God; Although I have cast them far off among the heathen, and although I have scattered them among the countries, yet I will be to them as a little sanctuary in the countries where they shall come. Therefore say, Thus saith the Lord God; I will even gather you from the people, and assemble you out of the countries where you have been scattered, and I will give you the land of Israel."

Again Moses says in Deut. 28: 36: "The Lord shall bring thee, and thy king which thou shalt set over thee unto a nation which neither thou nor thy fathers have known; and there shalt thou serve other gods, wood and stone." Here Moses says that Israel and the king they shall set over them shall be carried away captive to another nation. And when we see this prophecy made four hundreds years before Israel had a king, we must admit that more than human wisdom foresaw that Israel would set up a king to rule over them, and that this king and people would be led into another nation.

Deuteronomy 28: 53-56 foretells the terrible trials at the siege of Jerusalem, that parents should eat their own children, which Josephus says was literally fulfilled fifteen hundred years after it was spoken. Again Moses says in verse 68: "And the Lord shall bring thee again into Egypt with ships, by the way whereof I spake unto thee: Thou shalt see it no more again: and there ye shall be sold unto your enemies for bondmen and bondwomen, and no man shall buy you." Josephus and other writers say that many of the Jews were carried into Egypt and sold into slavery—thus fulfilling the prophecy of Moses in every particular. Many other prophecies in the Old Testament might be referred to, but as they are mainly repetitions of Moses' prophecy concerning Israel, it is necessary to refer to the fact that all the suffering that Israel endured was on account of disobeying the law of God. The Bible shows that when Israel obeyed, their peace and prosperity abounded everywhere; but when they disobeyed, sorrow and trouble fell upon them till they were finally cut off and scattered among all nations.

We now call attention to the prophecies concerning the Messiah, which are the most numerous and remarkable found in the Scriptures. In fact all the types and shadows of the Old Testament are prophetic in character, pointing to Christ and the church.

The first prophecy concerning the Messiah is found in Genesis 3: 15. The seed of the woman was to bruise the serpent's head. This prophecy is more in reference to the character and work of Christ than to his person. It gives us a clear idea of the contest between good and evil; that in all future time the children of the woman, led by the promised Teacher, should contend against sin and wickedness in the world, and finally with truth and righteousness triumph in a victory which will bruise the serpent's head and destroy his power. But the point in this prophecy plainly seen is the opposition between good and evil, between the righteous and disobedient, between those who serve God and those who serve him not.

This same prophecy is continued to Abraham in Genesis 12: 3: "In thee shall all the families of the earth be blessed." The promise is continued to Jacob, Genesis 49: 10: "The scepter shall not depart from Judah, nor a lawgiver from between his feet, until Shiloh come; and unto him shall the gathering of the people be." The important point in this prophecy is that the tribe of Judah should hold the scepter as God's peculiar people until the Savior should come. We know that the ten tribes were long before scattered among the nations, yet the tribe of Judah remained and his princes ruled in the temple service till the Savior came and the city was destroyed by the Romans. No human wisdom knowledge could foresee that the tribe of Judah would remain a distinct tribe for hundreds of years after all the other tribes were lost. It is clear evidence that divine power and wisdom is the author of Scripture prophecy.

There are other prophecies that the Messiah should come of the house of David; that he should be born in Bethlehem, Micah 5: 2; and of his death and resurrection, Psalm 16: 10.

The calling of the Gentile people is prophesied in Isaiah 42: 1-7. We know that this was literally fulfilled many hundred years after Isaiah had spoken it. We see the Gentiles called unto the covenant promised in Jeremiah 31: 31: "I will make a new covenant with the house of Israel and with the house of Judah." This prophecy shows that the first covenant is taken away from Israel and another made on better promises, into which the Gentiles are called. We know that these prophecies are fulfilled in the clearest manner. The language of the Savior in Matthew 21: 43, "The kingdom of God shall be taken from you and given to a nation bringing forth the fruits thereof," is another prophecy on the same point.

[This sermon is taken from Brother Robert's own manuscript, which evidently does not contain the entire discourse as he gave it.]

## INTERNAL EVIDENCE OF THE TRUTH OF CHRISTIANITY.

(Delivered at Mt. Morris, Ill., Jan. 10, 1892. Next to his last sermon.)

In the 16th and 17th verses of the 7th chapter of John you find our text: " Jesus answered them, and said, My doctrine is not mine, but his that sent me. If any man will do his will, he shall know of the doctrine, whether it be of God or whether I speak of myself." There are other texts which have similar language and express similar thoughts, bringing the same subject before the mind. Paul, writing to Timothy, says: " Take heed to thyself and to the doctrine and continue in them, and thou shalt save thyself and them that hear thee."

It is on account of the word *doctrine,* or the idea of doctrine as presented in our text, that we have selected this scripture and call your attention to it. The internal evidence of the truth of all Christianity is founded in its doctrine, or its truth as we term it.

The doctrine of the Bible is God's will revealed or manifested to man, and that doctrine and spirit and truth and will of God, revealed in the Bible, constitute the strongest evidence there is of the truth of the Bible. The reason we present doctrine in this form is because it is that doctrine we would keep before your minds during all of our sermons.

In bringing this evidence of the doctrine and truth and spirit of the Christian religion before your minds, we propose tonight to work from the external or outer manifestation of the truth, back into its origin. We look from without where we live, to within where God's truth must dwell.

The first point to which we call your attention is in creation. We go back to the Author of our being, the Author of the universe, the first Cause of all things, whom we call God. We affirm that the Creator and Author of all organization, in heaven and in earth, must be the Author of truth; that he must be the Author of that doctrine in will and mind and law, which brings to all his creatures their happiness and enjoyment.

We go to creation because we find there the works of God. He made the beasts of the field, the fowls of the air, the fishes of the sea, the heavens and the earth. By his almighty hand were built all the worlds that move in the universe of space. By studying the work of creation, man certainly can learn something of that God who is the Author of it all. That we may get correct ideas and knowledge from the study of creation, we call your attention more particularly to God's work in our own world.

He created the beasts of the field, with their natures and wants, the fowls of the air, with their natures and wants, and the fishes of the sea, with their natures and wants. When we think about God's work in making these creatures with their natures, their wants and the laws that govern them, we ask: Whence comes their happiness? The answer must be, "The great God who made them made the fountain from which flows all their happiness."

We behold the "cattle upon a thousand hills," feeding upon the green pastures, and we know that these pastures were made to satisfy their wants and to bring them all the happiness their nature is capable of enjoying. We discover that the Author of their being created the fountain from which arises all of their happiness.

We see the air filled with happy birds, winging their flight heavenward, and ask: Whence comes their happiness? The answer again must be, the same God that made them, with their powers, filled a fountain through which he pours out happiness upon them.

We turn to the mighty deep, teeming with God's creatures, and find that their natures are met and that all of their wants are supplied from the great fountain which he, who created them, gives to them.

Hence the answer to the great problem before the mind concerning all of these creatures with their God-given wants and natures is that the great God, who has created them all, has also made provision for their happiness and enjoyment.

This learned, we are ready for another step in the study of creation. We look down into the bowels of the earth and think of the deposits of silver and gold, iron and lead, the beds of coal and the fountains of oil and gas, and we say at once, all these minerals were not made for the beasts of the field, the birds of the air and the monsters of the deep. The green pastures, the aerial region and the briny deep were made for them and there they rejoice, but what in the work of the Creator were the birds of the air made for? A moment's thought and I conclude they were made for a being of a higher nature—one that has knowledge and intelligence, one with mind developed in harmony with the laws of nature and science. Thus skilled, I see man go down and bring up the ore, convert it into iron, stretch it across the continent, place chariots of his own construction upon it, and ride as it were, on the wings of the wind; and I know these minerals were not created for the beasts of the field, but for beings that can utilize them and thus enjoy this part of God's creation. And when I see man stretch the cable across the bed of the great ocean, and talk with his brother more than three thousand miles away, with the speed of the lightning's flash, I am led to ask: Did the God who created that mind with all its capacities for culture and development, and the laws which govern the activities of its several faculties in the exercise necessary to their growth—did that same God also create an inexhaustible fountain somewhere, from which this "wonderfully made" mind and soul may drink and be satisfied and happy?

But we want you to think a little farther. We borrow an illustration. A man puts a lion into a cage and feeds him with grass; but instead of living and thriving upon the grass he dwindles away and dies. Why? The wants of his nature were not supplied. The pinch of hunger led to a miserable death. He then puts another lion into the cage and feeds him upon meat. He grows and thrives and is happy. Why? Because the keeper knows his wants and has supplied the lion with that which meets his wants and he rejoices in all the capacities of his being. He then illustrates further by putting a lamb into a cage and feeds it upon meat, the food on which the lion flourished, and it dwindles and dies. Why? Because the wants of its nature were not supplied. But now he takes another lamb and turns it into green pastures, the food God made to meet the wants of its nature. It grows and thrives.

Now I want you to note that the green pasture is like the truth to that lamb. If there is truth for the lamb, it is in the green pastures, because happiness to its utmost capacity grows out of its wants being supplied by that truth? And if there is falsehood to that lamb at all, it is in the meat, because it makes an utter failure to supply its wants. So with the lion. Now this is true everywhere throughout the mighty empire of God, that same truth stands, that whatever brings to God's creatures the greatest happiness they can enjoy, is truth to them as certain as they exist. On the other hand that which destroys their happiness is falsehood to them. Man may say what he pleases, we know it is falsehood to the lion and the lamb when their wants are not met.

Now while this is true, we want you to keep it in mind throughout all of our investigations. And the next question that we call your attention to is: Has this God, this Creator who has made all this, has he made a religion for the mind and soul and body of man? Has this God filled the great fountain of truth to supply all the wants of the man in the form of a religion, a doctrine, a law of truth and righteousness, that will bring to man all of his happiness? The God who made the eye made the light as a condition necessary to vision. The God who made the ear made the sound for a similar purpose. The God who made the mind created all the laws in nature and science necessary to the development of that mind. Did that same God make a religion? Did he make or give a system or doctrine of truth to man in his mind and spirit that can bring all the happiness and all the enjoyment that man's nature is capable of? If he did, it must be his religion and it is as much a truth to him as if God had made that which can bring to man all the happiness he is capable of enjoying. If God has given to our world that which will satisfy the wants of a man's mind when it is developed, and of man's soul, body and spirit, he has given us the doctrine and truth of our text, that if we do his will, we shall know that it is of God. We know it because it brings to us all of the happiness that it is possible for our nature and condition to enjoy in this world and the world to come. And when we get that, we know it is the truth to us. And if there is a doctrine or if there is a religion, if there is anything presented to man that destroys his happiness, I tell you without hesitating, it is not the truth. Give a man intemperance and profanity and gambling and all kindred vices, and ask me whether the things ruling him are truth to him and I answer, No. If there is falsehood in earth or heaven or hell, it has hold of him. I know it because it has destroyed his happiness and the happiness of all those around him. The internal evidence of Christanity is the strongest possible testimony that can be given.

Now we assume that God did give to the world a religion, and when God gave the world a religion he did not give it the worst one. God never made the worst one, nor the next to the worst, nor even the one next to that. When God gave the world a religion, he gave it the best one, and it was not only best, but it was a perfect one. It is so remarkable that it has fed the soul, body and spirit with all the happiness that it could enjoy. Let us make a little comparison.

Robert Ingersoll says that all religions are alike. Now I do not think he told the truth, or came anywhere near to it. I believe there is just as much difference between religions as the distance is from heaven to hell. This is a pretty strong expression, but let us look at it. Here is idolatry. What is idolatry? An idol is that which a man conceives in his own mind, or makes with his own hands and calls it a god; that which he has formed in his mind, and then sets up and falls down and worships. Think about that. Can a man make an idol, a god, better than himself? Did you ever see a stream rise above its source? A man who by nature, is so bad a sinner that language can scarcely describe his condition, makes a god and then falls down and worships it! A god is no better than the man who makes it and can never make the man any better. And I will tell you why. When man makes an idol and says it is a god, that god is in his imagination, and the more devoutly he worships it, the more he becomes like it and the more it gets into him.

Suppose he worships the lion. Suppose he worships it forty years, or threescore years and ten, and becomes just like the lion, he will be no higher, no better, no purer than when he began. Why? Because there is nothing there to raise him higher or make him better and purer. There is nothing there to raise him higher than his own nature. Idolatry never did; it never can raise a man above his own fallen and lost condition, because when the man makes a god, the poor god is no better than the poor man, and the more he worships the poor god, the more the man sinks into sin and wickedness. History proves this to be correct.

Go to nations that have worshiped idols for thousands of years. Go to China for example. They worshiped idols for centuries, and today they butcher Christian men and women and children as they would brutes. No conscience, no soul, hardly at all. Four thousand years of idolatry didn't raise them at all, because there is nothing in an idol better than the man; and how can he become better by worshiping it? That is not all. It is not the worst. Idolatry has in it another idea. It is this: Idolaters make their gods according to their ideas of sin, that their gods may take care of them while engaged in their wickedness and sin. For instance, the drunkard may have the god of Bacchus. He does not have that god for the purpose of making him a sober man at all, but he worships that god so that when he is intoxicated, his god will take care of him. The thought of idolatry never comprises the idea that you must quit your sins and turn away from them in order to please the god. It is not in the system. The principle of idolatry is that by worshiping your god, you may appease his wrath and thus have him to protect you in your sins. Now, when Robert Ingersoll says that all religions are alike, he is mistaken, because the religion of Christ is precisely opposite to idolatry. Christ says you must turn away from your sins. He says to the drunkard, you must cease drinking and become converted, you must turn around and go the other way. You must quit sinning. You see the difference in the religion of Jesus Christ. All the idolatrous worship in the world has nothing in it that can make a man any better.

Among other ungodly practices belonging to idolatry is the treatment of woman. Her condition under idolatry is a miserable one. Now we know that through the influence of the Chinese, idolatry has come to our own land, but they have come into this Christian land through the violation of law. The husband has sold his wife and the father has sold his daughter to be the wife of another. He takes the privilege to sell her whenever he desires to do so, even in our own country. It is because of this that we do not want them in our country. They bring idolatry here. The condition of woman where idolatry reigns is a strong evidence against it, according to our rule or doctrine. Look at her condition in those countries where idolatry is the religion. I have here a report from some of the English military officers of the East India Islands, where idolatry reigns largely. When those islands came under the control of England, she sent her army there and I have a report of some of the British officers regarding the condition of the people there, under idolatry.

There was the river Ganges, worshiped by the Hindoos, and there the mothers cast their infants into the jaws of the crocodile. Now I ask the question, can that be the truth to that infant? Can it be the truth to that mother? Is it truth that takes her children and throws them into the river Ganges? To cast her first-born into the jaws of the sea monster, I ask, is that the truth to that mother? Is it the truth to that child? I reply that if there is falsehood in the universe, I know this is falsehood to that mother and to that infant. There is enough internal evidence of the destruction of happiness and life to show that idolatry is falsehood to both.

But now to Christianity. It does turn men away

from sin. It is exactly the opposite of idolatry. But what is the reason it turns men away from sin? Think a moment. In our first sermon it was God in all his righteousness and wisdom and holiness and love manifested in Christ. We hold him up today as the object of worship. We see there is holiness, righteousness, wisdom and love, and all the attributes of a loving God in perfection. We ask you to look at Jesus, the Author and Finisher of faith. To look to him, God's own Son. Look to him as the Redeemer, look to him as the wisdom and power of God. We ask you to think of him a moment. Turn that man away from the idol, and have him look to Jesus and his righteousness. You take that man; he cannot look to Jesus honestly and sincerely without being benefited. When the religion of Jesus is before the mind, and he is devoutly worshiping Jesus according to the Scriptures, that religion gets into his nature, and the more he looks at it, the more he is moulded like it.

Take a little child and put him into a saloon, let him be raised there, hearing the vulgarity and the profanity, witnessing the conduct of that den of vice, and it will become a part of his life. You will hear him swearing upon the streets almost as soon as he can lisp the name of God in vain. Why? It has been before his mind and has gotten into his heart. You place him before sin and idolatry and it gets into his heart. Again, you place a man under the influence of Christ, bring his righteousness and holiness before his mind, and the more devoutly he looks, the more his heart will become filled with holiness and goodness. That is why the Scriptures teach such sacred language: "Look unto me all the ends of the earth and be saved, for I am God and there is none other." Look to him.

The righteousness that is revealed in God is Christianity. That will bring goodness and peace and joy to the children of men; everything to make you happy. The idea represented in our text, that the doctrines and truths that are revealed in Christ, getting into your hearts, are the doctrines and truths revealed in him for you to worship. We say we have the right to make this demand of you; that you should look to Jesus in his life and in his humility, and in his love, his kindness, in his death and his burial, in the resurrection and ascension. Look to him in all the glory that God has given, and worship him as your God. With your devotion centered upon his life, let it get into your heart, as the doctrine and the faith, and the spirit and the power. Because the tendency is to make you better and they are sure to succeed in their work.

Take that truth to man. Let it come to his mind and soul and spirit in the world of wickedness and sin and sorrow and death. You ask if it will meet his wants, and if you cannot answer it, let me take you to the Hindoo mother, casting her child into the mouth of a crocodile. Let Jesus get hold of that mother, let her embrace his doctrine, his truth and spirit. A world of difference! He will take that little child up in his arms and bless it and tell the mother that of such is the kingdom of heaven, and take it back and bring it up in the nurture and admonition of the Lord. Teach it by precept and example. God's truth revealed in Christ. Go and tell that mother, and not only that mother but also the child, that to both of them God has revealed his doctrine, the doctrine that you can enjoy, the one that you are at liberty to embrace. A religion that will spare the child that it may live with its mother, to help hold her up and take care of her, to spare the mother that she may bring up the child. Make a comparison if you can. The one that rescues that mother and that child is truth. The opposite is falsehood.

Go to that infant that Williams speaks of, and there stand by and witness. Her mother is sacrificing her life on the pile that burns her father. Putting the torch to the pile that burns the bodies, and makes the children orphans! Does that meet their wants? As I told you before, we know it does not. But turn over to the religion of Jesus. It would take the mother off the pile and give her back to the children, and the glorious Gospel of Jesus would raise them up in his righteousness. We want you to get the idea of the contrast that is made between idolatry and its teachings and the religion of Jesus Christ, so far as the internal evidence is concerned. The one that brings the greatest happiness to man, I am sure, is the one that is the truth. That is the truth and that which destroys your happiness is error and falsehood to you. Young man, if you are running into sin, against the counsel of your father, of your mother, who have sent you here,—contrary to the counsel and desire of your teachers,—if you are running into sin, that sin is destroying your happiness. I know that it is error. I know that it is falsehood. But if you are obeying your parents in the Lord, if you are obeying the Gospel and living according to the righteousness revealed in Jesus Christ, I know that you are happy tonight. Your professors, your fathers and your mothers are rejoicing because of you. They thank God for you. The very thought brings joy and happiness to them.

Now let us get a little closer to the thought, if we can. You take what the Savior and the apostles, the Spirit of God and the Gospel teaches children, the young man and the young woman. Now is not that the greatest instruction you can get? Can you add anything to it? What God's Word teaches children in regard to their happiness, obeying their parents, etc., the teachings in regard to how parents shall treat their children,—and you cannot improve upon it. You may take God's teachings to the husband, how he is to treat his wife, and it is as far from idolatry as heaven is from earth. He is not to sell her for fifty dollars, but to study the teachings of Christ as to how he shall love her. You could not buy her for one hundred and fifty dollars. No sir, a thousand worlds like this would be no temptation at all. Why? The goodness of God has got hold of that family. Their happiness is more than dollars and cents.

Therefore my argument comes that the internal

evidence of the Bible brings the greatest happiness that is possible for any man to enjoy, whether he be rich or poor, small or great, well or sick,—no difference when, whether he be living or dead. I know that is truth. Reasoning from the outside I see into the fountain. I know that a man of God today has happiness and feelings. When he thinks about himself and about his former condition, and what God has done for him, and the blessings he has conferred upon him, he realizes a happiness and an enjoyment in his soul that the sinner cannot enjoy. Though you bind him in chains, you cannot destroy it. You may take all of his property and his health, take him to where Paul would go, to Nero's block, there is no chance to destroy him.

I want to take the subject a little farther. While God has revealed this truth, in all its applications to individuals, as we have seen, he also revealed it to the church. He has organized in that church the spirit and doctrine, and truth, and righteousness which he has revealed, for ruling and controlling and governing the brethren and sisters, to make them happy. God has made that church for whom? Let me tell you that he has not only made it for the members in the church, those who have been converted and regenerated, but he has made it as a dwelling place and the home for their children, and for their neighbors, and for their friends and of those around them. The church is a place of worship, to which we all can go, and to which we can call even sinners, that they may come and live, to come and see and hear, and know of God's righteousness and truth. Ah! the kingdom and church that God organized here for father and mother, the brothers and sisters, all in one company, to gather up and to go into the service of God, is where God put the greatest truth, for the greatest possible happiness.

Let us contrast: That is the institution that God has made for you and me to live in. The world is full of secret societies and other societies. You find secret societies for almost everything. They have organized some for one thing and some for another. They have organized until the husband goes, I don't know where, or what it is for, but he goes out and stays possibly until midnight. It may not be a secret society, it may be a political club, a social club or a gathering where men may go. The husband leaves his wife and children home at night. I am not quite fast enough. They have gotten up societies for women, too, and the husband will go to one society and the wife to another, and turn the children out into the street.

Let us look at religion. Let us look at the church. It will take the husband in, it will take the wife in, the father and mother. Not only them but it will also gather up the children and take them into the church as well. I am glad we are not above taking our children to meeting. If the people just let the mother take care of them, I am always satisfied. But get the idea that when God makes up this church, he makes it up for the greatest possible happiness. Father and mother, son and daughter may here meet. We say to you, brethren and sisters, it is for the greatest amount of happiness that you can enjoy. Go to that great truth which God has made to supply your soul, body and spirit. God has made that organization.

Gather up the truth of our text, tonight, father and mother, son and daughter, gather up the truth that God has revealed. Take them home with you and keep them in your heart, and I tell you they will bring you joy and happiness and peace, the greatest that you can have while in this world and in the world to come.

Another thought and then we are through. The Spirit leads in all this doctrine. The Spirit of God is the fountain from which it comes. The Father sent his Son. He came into the world. He fulfilled the work that God gave him to do and he went back and sent the Spirit in his stead. The Spirit is here now dwelling with you and me, the Spirit leads those today and guides those who are led by the Spirit. "They are the sons of God," Paul said. The Spirit of God led the church eighteen hundred years ago, in their worship and service, in their enjoyments and in their happiness. It led them into the entire fellowship of that religion of God in Christ, to shine out into the world.

And may God help us is our prayer.

## THE SPIRIT AS A WITNESS.

(Delivered in Brethren's Chapel, Huntingdon, Pa., 1880. From this text, Brother Robert preached his last sermon at Mt. Morris, Ill., Jan. 11, 1892.)

"The Spirit itself beareth witness with our spirit that we are the children of God." Rom. 8: 16.

The language of our text brings us rather to a doctrinal discourse this morning, which we promise by the help of God to bring before your minds. We think it probable that we will speak to you again today and we will try to make our other discourse more practical; that in the two discourses we may get instruction that will, at least some of it, be adapted to the mind and condition of every one here this morning. Hence a little doctrine in my remarks may be of benefit, and on that account we beg your careful attention, because it requires more thought to get a thorough and full understanding of doctrinal questions than it does of subjects of a more practical nature. Our text is one, you can see at once, that is impressive and is most difficult to comprehend fully when brought before our minds. It is the subject of the Spirit. It is of what you are and what God is beyond the manifestation of what we can see in the physical organization of matter. Hence the subject is full of all there is of importance, belonging to what man is and what man ever will be.

We think we know less about spirits and spiritual existence than we really do; we think the subject more difficult than it really is. It is true the subject is too grand and great and deep and high for the mind of man to comprehend it fully, but it is also true that man can know a great deal about himself, and in the text before us, we get information concerning him which is of eternal importance. We can know of spirits and spiritual existence as we can know of anything else that has to be manifested to us. We can find the organization of any character.

For illustration, you can know something of the life of anything real to see that life manifested in the physical organization that develops it. You can have a pretty good knowledge of that something when you see it in its development. If you see the organization fully developed, you can look back beyond it, until you run down the life and power that produced it. It is true your research is limited, but much you can know about your own life. So it is with the subject before us. Of the Spirit of God and the spirit of man we can know much. We can see it manifested in man, and from that manifestation we can go back to the cause and to the bottom from which it originated, and from the knowledge received much benefit and instruction can be gained. Then when we come to the subject of the Spirit of God, bearing witness to our spirits that we are the children of God, we are having really an important subject. As the light and power that produces all physical organization around us is seen and read in its manifestation, so spirit is seen and read in the manifestation of mind: You see mind, and nothing before you is greater in its worth and value than it is; and when you behold the mind, you are only getting at the manifestation of the spirit that is within you. Mind is dependent upon spirit, as the tree is dependent upon its light for growth. The mind belongs to spirit and not to matter. Physical organization of matter cannot produce mind. It is too high for that little fountain. Mind is not dependent upon matter but is built upon spirit. Paul understood that subject when he said, " God knoweth what is in the mind of the Spirit "; not in the mind of man. The body has no mind but " God knoweth what is in the mind of the Spirit." " The Spirit searcheth all things, yea the deep things of God." Listen to Paul again when he says: " For what man knoweth the things of man, save the spirit of man which is in him? even so, the things of God knoweth no man, but the Spirit of God." "The natural mind cannot discern the things of the Spirit "; that is, not man's physical organization, not his natural power, anything belonging to him this side of Spirit, cannot discern spiritual things. In him there is no spiritual discernment.

Then another idea connected with the subject is, that the Bible that saves man must be spiritual. It must be a religion that reaches the spirit of man. The Spirit of God communicates with the spirit of man, gives the understanding and knowledge. This belongs to the Spirit and belongs to men on earth and angels in heaven. We see in the universe of God, angels and men. When they meet on earth; in Eden, or in the plains of Moriah, or when they meet in heaven, the extent of knowledge and conversation between them comes of mind, and the understanding and thought gives itself spirit. Then we will look at the subject of man as brought out in our text, that the Spirit of God beareth witness with the spirit of man, to prove that he is the child of God. You get the idea presented. What is it that belongs to a witness? It is beginning the special work of the mind, and in which to bear witness. Hence on this subject we see that the Apostle Paul comes with the idea that the spirit of man and the Spirit of God both witness with the other. It is upon this that they both have knowledge. We make these remarks to show you that we believe in a religion that is spiritual. We want it put on its true spiritual basis, and we want you to understand that no relation of God reaches the spiritual but what is spiritual. Your fellowship, union and communion with God is spiritual. "The Spirit of God beareth witness with our spirits." Don't understand him to mean that the Spirit of God only bears witness *to* our spirits but *with* our spirits. How much greater the idea of our spirits being brought in harmony with God's Spirit, and in communion and fellowship with the great Spirit of God. It is the grandest thought of the universe, to talk of a weak mortal as you and I being brought into harmony, union and oneness with the great Spirit, and witness with it as we witness with one another. It bears witness with our spirits to prove that we are the children of God. What is the witness for? It is to prove something. It is to prove that we are the children of God, the greatest truth to be proven in the world. You may think it worth but little here, but over yonder it is important.

Witness now the truth that we are the children of God. It is like a trial in court, to decide whether this man or another be the legal heir to the greatest inheritance in the universe. But God's Spirit is not witness to an estate of that kind, but to an inheritance such as is figured in the text, witnessing to prove that you are the heir to that inheritance, and these two witnesses, bearing witness one with the other to prove that you are God's children. The thing is proven. That settles the heirship throughout all eternity, and that settles the harmony of God's Spirit and your spirit, and witnessing one with another. Suppose the witnesses could not agree, could not support the testimony of the other, and when the testimony of one would be given it would be right the reverse of the other. If one witness would contradict the other the cause would be lost, and the inheritance a failure. One witness should corroborate the testimony of the other. That is the idea presented in the figure of the text. If the Spirit of God and our spirits do not bear witness one with the other; if there is a contradiction; if there is a departure from the truth; if there is not, as our text says there should be, a witness one with the other, then the great truth of our text is not proven.

The idea of our text is something like this: Should I tell you that I have a son that is a preacher, that in every way you could imagine his preaching proves that he is my son; that his very spirit is the witness with my spirit; that his countenance, that his gestures, that his voice, his faith and practice all bear witness that he is my son; that the witness one with the other is the testimony that will prove to you that he is the son of Robert H. Miller. Suppose that the young man just looked like me, and in everything bore witness to what I said, that it was in perfect harmony, there would be no doubt at all that he was my son. You get the idea. I presume now the point with the apostles was, among other things, that if God's Spirit bore witness with our spirits that we are his children, we ought to be like the Father. And why does that idea come out so clear here? Because you would expect the children to be like their father. It is because those who are born of the Spirit, those who are born of God, should be, as our text says, the children of God. And those who are not his children should become like him, and should bear witness with the other, proving that they are the children of God. What power, what influence, what blessedness and happiness do we find in that idea of our text! That in order to save man, in order to fit and qualify him for heaven, and that the influence and power of Satan might be destroyed, God would come in the influence and power of his own Son, that we should be born again, made over in our spirit, that we should be converted to God and that we should be joined to him. Being in harmony with God, in all his Word, in all his works, in all his providence, in all his truth and in the words of our text, that God's Spirit is bearing witness with our spirits every day, in our faith, in our practice and in all our hopes. In all our efforts and purposes, God's Spirit bears witness with our spirit that we are the children of God. We are brought into harmony and oneness and union with the great Spirit that has created us, and who rules the universe and reigns in the heavens eternal. That God is the Author of that reasonable and glorious system of saving us, by making a salvation that is sure. It cannot fail.

You may talk on any subject of the Gospel, its commands, its faith, its practice, and the great truth of our text, that the Spirit of God bears witness with our spirits is the great thought manifested. It is the great idea presented that in the divine revelation, God's Spirit and our spirits must come in harmony. Talk on the subject of baptism, and to get at the truth you only need to get the idea of our text, that our spirits must get in harmony with the Spirit of God. True conversion and preparation of man for fellowship with God is that which brings his spirit into perfect harmony with the Spirit of God, until they both witness the same thing.

Suppose God's Witness is brought, and we come up to examine ourselves and we find our testimony, the witness of our spirits contradicts it; that it changes the witness of God's Spirit; suppose for instance the witness of God's Spirit on the subject of baptism conflicts with the witness of our own spirits on the same subject, how dangerous the testimony! It would not be as God would have it. The idea of our text is that God's Spirit bears witness with our spirits on the whole plan of salvation. Thank God it is the whole truth in his Witness. Could we get all the grandeur of this text in our own lives, and feel that our spirits are brought in harmony with the Spirit of God, and that these spirits of ours bear witness with God's Spirit on every subject, we then probably would more fully comprehend its meaning.

I will yet present another point to you. I have lost my companion and nearly all of my children. Under the providence affliction has been long and deep in my family. If my spirit can be brought in harmony with the Spirit of God, the Great Spirit that rules the universe, the Great Spirit that has created and made me, the Great Spirit that must redeem me and save me at last, if I can get into harmony in the works of that Spirit, in his providences, in his ways and in his infinite wisdom; if I can live there, I may stand rejoicing, because my spirit beats in harmony with the Spirit of God. The idea of our text, that the "Spirit of God bears witness with our spirits," is illustrated in the Christian under affliction. He travels through life with seeming numberless trials hanging upon him, and every step he takes seems to bring him more; but when we look at that man and see his spirit bright and shining, we know that it is in harmony with the Great Spirit that leads him. He bears witness with the Great Spirit and the Great Spirit with his spirit and we know nothing can destroy that witness. What a power and influence came out of the spirit of the Apostle Paul; and the Spirit of God and Paul's spirit witnessed one with another. You get the idea then of our text, that our spirits bear witness with God's Spirit, and this brings happiness and joy while here in this pilgrimage, and when we come to die and to cross the river of death, it will be a rod and a staff to comfort us.

One more thought in regard to the subject and then we are done. The apostle says God's Spirit bears witness with our spirit to prove that we are the children of God. Don't get too limited an idea of this subject. This is a relationship that we want enjoyed by you all. And oh, we want more than that. We want the fact that we are the children of God proven to the world. God is bearing witness with our spirits, proving to the world that we are the children of God. There should be sufficient in your lives to convince the world that you are the children of God. How important that our lives as individuals, that our actions and conduct, all together should be a witness before the world, proving that we are the children of God! There should be harmony. Oh! If God would give his own Son as a Witness; if in God's Spirit there was so much love, that he would give his only Son to save the world, our spirits should come in harmony with that Spirit. We should know that Spirit; get the power of that Spirit, and work as God did for the salvation of men.

This gives us the idea of our work. This gives us the idea of our spiritual relation to God. It should ever lead us beyond the mere pursuit of earthly things. It should turn us to the immortal Spirit that lives eternal; that makes our fellowship and communion with God. It should turn us to our race and help us to look at it. We may see them drunk and degraded in every form, and we may probably turn away with a feeling of indifference. But don't do that! There is a spark of divinity in all men, however debased, and it is your duty to bring them back to the image and likeness of God. Bring your spirits, desires, affections and energies all in harmony with the Spirit of God, and prove to the world that you are his children, and let every effort be put forth to save sinners. May God bless and enable you to gather up the indifferent, and take them with you, and bring them into a practical relationship with God, is my prayer.

## CHAPTER X.

### Later Life and Death.

When we closed the direct narrative of Brother Robert's life in chapter one, his home had been broken up. The mother had gone to join her four children on the other side of the river. The father and four children were left to mourn the departure of the dear ones for eternity. A mother's love and care were gone, and without this there can be no happy home. For one and a half years the family circle was thus incomplete. Then it was re-established by an event of which D. P. Saylor tells the readers of the *Gospel Preacher*, Sept. 27, 1881:

"Married,—By Elder D. P. Saylor, on Thursday, Sept. 15, 1881, at the home of the bride's mother near Ladiesburg, Md., Elder R. H. Miller, of Ashland City, Ashland County, Ohio, and Sister Emma Norris, of Frederick County, Maryland.

"While we regret the loss of our dear sister from among us, we congratulate our Brother Miller in his happy choice of so amiable a sister for his wife. Our best wishes and prayers go with her to her new home in Ohio, where she will be a comfort to her husband and a light to the church. God bless the happy pair. D. P. S."

After a few months of happy married life at Ashland, Brother Robert resigned the presidency of the college and editorship of the *Gospel Preacher*. Soon after this he made arrangements to move to North Manchester, Ind. To this place he moved his family in the spring of 1882. After a short residence in the city, he moved to a farm which the brethren assisted him to buy.

His task in the North Manchester church was no easy one to perform. There were all classes of members, from radical Old Order Brethren to radical progressives. It was just at that period when both extreme elements were leaving the church. How to handle a church of some three hundred members, where such conditions prevailed, was a serious question. As it was, the church at North Manchester lost many members; with a less skillful leader the loss would have been much greater. His unquestioned loyalty to the church and his broad-minded views had their influence on all.

As an elder he was a success. He was mild, but firm. He was able to grasp both sides of any trouble and was generally successful in bringing opposing parties together. He was not a partisan in any case, and so rarely failed to keep the respect of all concerned. He had views too broad to be servile to rigid rules of discipline.

As a leader, he never desired to go faster than he could take the body of the church with him. With him the great question was union. How to keep that and yet sacrifice no gospel principle was the question that most concerned him in directing his church. That his work was successful can be judged from the fact that at the time of his death

## LATER LIFE AND DEATH

the North Manchester congregation was one of the strongest and most loyal churches in the Brotherhood.

In the Middle District of Indiana he was everywhere loved and respected. To the elders of that District he was as a father. To him they looked for advice, and even today his counsels are followed by many bishops who once were associated with him and received his lessons. He was not, however, independent in thought and action, but often went to his brethren for advice and help. He repeatedly served as moderator of district meeting and was nearly always chosen to help settle trouble in churches. He seemed to have reduced church government to a science of which he was thoroughly acquainted with all its problems.

Brother Robert was highly respected in the community in which he lived, both by the members and those out of the church. When he lived at Ladoga it was said that he could hardly get out of town, after being absent from home, because of his many friends who desired to talk with him. He had few real intimate friends, though all reverenced him because of his noble character and superior wisdom. At North Manchester his most intimate associates were two brethren in the laity, Daniel Horning and Abram Miller. The latter is still living at the ripe old age of eighty-five. They probably understood him better than any one else outside his family. He often visited his near neighbors. He seldom stayed long, but he had a good, cheerful conversation while he did stay.

He was a master of interesting and profitable conversation. He was well informed on most subjects and took delight in talking with others on matters of interest to them. He had the enviable reputation of being able to teach his hearers something every time they listened to him. He was witty but did not try to impress the fact upon his hearers. He said but few idle words. In repartee he was hard to put at disadvantage. On one occasion some one accused him of being a strict constructionist because of his technical manner of looking at the contents of a query. His immediate reply was, " I would rather be a strict-constructionist than a latitudinarian."

As a farmer he was a success. He could take as much interest in his farm as he could in other work. One of the merchants at North Manchester declared that there was more grain raised on Robert Miller's eighty acres than any other farm of like size in the community. It was only his extensive church labors that prevented him from reaping financial rewards from the farm. The pity is that he was not wholly supported by the church, that it had not been necessary to wear out his body in daily toil, but that the church might have received the full strength of his many-sided genius.

His life in the home was that of an ideal father and husband. His kindness, patience, self-sacrifice and tender sympathy were all that could be asked of any one. Whatever reverses came, he met them with patience and calm resignation. In hours of sickness he was strong and brave to endure, even

"The old Meetinghouse, two miles west of North Manchester, where the Annual Meeting was held in 1878 and where Elder R. H. Miller did most of his preaching during the last ten years of his life."

## LATER LIFE AND DEATH

when death strokes were falling so heavily upon his dear ones.

To his second union there were born five sons, one of whom died in infancy. To these boys he was devotedly attached and his last thoughts were concerning them. Their names in order of their ages are, Oliver, Daniel, Robert and John. The brave mother has kept her little band together. For a few years after her husband's death she continued to reside on the farm near North Manchester. Then feeling the need of having some one to help teach the boys farming, she moved on the farm of her brother-in-law, Elder Samuel Stoner, near Ladoga, Ind. Here they lived until the boys were grown; then a farm was purchased a few miles distant. Here the companion and sons of our dear brother reside at present.

About two years before his death, Brother Robert moved his family from the farm to a little home near the west house in the North Manchester congregation. He was now relieved of the duties of the farm and could be more closely connected with the church work. Among the last of his loving deeds was assisting in building a new house for worship. The old house became too poor and inconvenient for further use. This was replaced by a large, commodious brick structure which still stands on the ground where the Anual Meeting of 1878 was held. Brother Robert was greatly interested in this new building. He was permitted to use it but little and his was one of the first funerals held in it.

His health during his last few years was not

good. Many engagements had to be canceled because of a lack of strength. For this reason, in his later life he was not so active as he had once been. He did little writing for the *Gospel Messenger* and held but three debates in ten years. He did not hold many series of meetings but was often called to officiate at funerals, marriages, special meetings and to preach doctrinal sermons.

It was for this purpose that the brethren at Mt. Morris, Ill., arranged for him to come to the special Bible Term in January, 1892, and deliver a series of doctrinal sermons. It was the intention to publish this series of sermons in a book for the edification of the church. Brother Robert realized the great opportunity offered him and the responsibility and possibility of his work. He accepted it gladly and put forth great effort in preparation. He began his work at Mt. Morris on the evening of January 8, 1892. Many brethren from far and near were present to hear this great champion of the faith defend its principles. Those who heard him say that he was at his best. But the work so auspiciously begun was soon cut short. The enthusiasm in preparation and the exertion in delivering his message were too straining on his weakened physical system. Tuesday, Jan. 12, found him sick in bed at the home of Brother J. G. Royer.

Other brethren filled the appointments with the hope that Brother Robert would soon be able to be with them again. But hope was in vain. The malady was seen to have a firm hold upon him. The wife was summoned to his bedside. Week after week went by. The whole Brotherhood watched, and waited, and prayed that the *Gospel Messenger* would bring more cheerful news from his bedside. Now their hopes would rise only to be dashed to the ground again. The fight for life was a losing one from the first and on March the 8th, shortly after 10 A. M., Elder Robert H. Miller passed from earthly labor to reward.

The closing scenes as well as the sad funeral rites were told to the readers of the *Gospel Messenger* by Elder D. L. Miller. We are giving the whole of his vivid account:

" During his illness it was our privilege to be with Brother Miller quite frequently. When we were at home, we sat with him almost daily, and we can truthfully say that, in all our experience, we never saw anyone bear sickness and suffering so uncomplainingly and so patiently as did he, and when he came to realize that the time of his departure was at hand, he met death as peacefully and as calmly as if he were simply ' folding the drapery of his couch about him and lying down to pleasant dreams.' He talked to us all quietly and calmly, making all necessary arrangements as to his business affairs, asking us to take charge of the further publication of his book, spoke of his desire to have his funeral conducted without ostentation or show, saying: ' Let it all be done in harmony with the principles of the church,' and in all his conversation he was just as calm as if he had been engaged in talking about some one else. He manifested no fear of death, but entered the valley trusting in the God of his salvation. He fell with his armor on, battling for the cause he loved so well.

"On the morning of his death the sun rose bright and clear. The clouds which had hung heavily overhead for several days had disappeared and it was a bright, beautiful morning. In the sick chamber lay our dear brother, the sands of his life almost run. His wan, sunken features told of the physical suffering he had endured. Around his bedside stood his sorrow-stricken wife and a number of brethren and sisters, who felt that a wise counselor, a father in Israel, a faithful servant of God, a loving brother was going away from them. A curtain at the window was drawn aside and the bright sunlight fell across his couch, but the light was too strong for his weakened eyes. The curtain was again replaced and then the question was asked, 'Is it not too dark?' and the sufferer said, 'It is light enough for me.' Yes, it was light enough for him, for in his soul was shining the light of the brightest hope that God gives his children in this world,—a light that gilds even the dark valley and shadow of death, and makes it but a pathway to glory. It was the hope of eternal life that cheered our brother, the hope of a mansion above; 'A building of God, an house not made with hands, eternal in the heavens.'

"Soon after this he requested that we have a season of worship and devotion around his bedside. He indicated the position to be occupied by those present, and being asked if he had a Scripture reading to suggest, after a moment's thought he gave these words: 'For we know that if our earthly house of this tabernacle were dissolved, we have a building of God, an house not made with hands, eternal in the heavens.' After prayer, to which he most heartily responded, he left messages to absent loved ones, and especially to his little boys who were so soon to be left fatherless. And then he composed himself and patiently waited for the end to come. He was ready and anxious to go home. As his feet were slipping o'er the brink, we heard the thrice-repeated prayer: 'Oh, that the Lord would come and take me,' and with these words upon his lips, the last he was ever to utter in this world, the Lord took him home. 'And he was not, for God took him.' Such was the death of our beloved R. H. Miller. A death like this must have inspired the prophet when he gave utterance to these words: 'Let me die the death of the righteous, and let my last end be like his.'

"After the memorial services, which were held in the chapel at this place, we started on our sad journey to North Manchester, Ind., the earthly home of our departed brother, and where he requested that his body might be placed in the tomb. The journey was a sad one. Only a short time before, our brother had come to us to labor in the ministry of the Word. Sickness had come to him, and then his devoted wife hastened to his bedside to care for him, and now we are going to his home with his lifeless body. While we were cheered by his glorious and triumphant death, yet we felt the personal loss which we all had sustained, and it was with sad hearts that we made the journey.

"We reached North Manchester in the evening in the midst of a heavy storm of wind and snow. A number of the brethren and sisters were at the depot, and in every face was to be seen the evidence of the love all bore for Brother Miller. Each one felt that in his death they had suffered a personal loss, and that his place would not be easily filled. Carriages were in waiting and we were taken to the now desolate home of Sister Miller, about two miles from North Manchester. The scene here was one to melt the hardest heart. The meeting between Sister Miller and her now fatherless boys we will not attempt to describe. It was a scene over which angels might well weep.

"The next day at eleven A. M., the funeral was appointed at the Brethren's new meetinghouse, which had only recently been completed, and in the construction of which Brother Miller had taken a great interest. The house is a very large one, yet notwithstanding the fact that the roads were very bad, and that a heavy snowstorm prevailed the entire day, the large meetinghouse was filled, thus showing that our brother had the respect of the community. Bro. J. G. Royer preached the funeral sermon. His text was taken from the chapter selected by our dear brother to be read the morning of his death, 2 Cor. 5:10: 'For we must all appear before the judgment seat of Christ; that every one may receive the things done in his body, according to that he hath done, whether it be good or bad.' The sermon was a practical lesson to the living, and was made especially impressive on account of the occasion that called it forth. At the close the dying words of Brother Miller to his children were repeated, and the scene was painfully impressive. A number of ministers were present from other congregations, and Brethren William R. Deeter, Amasa Puterbaugh and the writer assisted Brother Royer in the services.

"We laid his body to rest in the silent grave, surrounded by a multitude of sorrowing friends, whose tears manifested the depth of their love and sorrow. Around that open grave the snow was eddying and drifting, driven by the fierce storm. As we stood there we thought of the quiet, peaceful rest our brother was then enjoying, in such contrast with the tempest that was raging all about us. Undisturbed by the driving storm, he sleeps his last sleep. The storms are past, the pains of death no more feared, life's labor and sorrow have ceased and the warfare is ended. His last battle has been fought. With his armor on, with his face to the foe, faithful unto death, he fell in the line of duty, and his soul has found rest and peace with God.

"'Servant of God, well done!
Rest from thy loved employ;
The battle fought, the victory won
Enter thy Master's joy.'

"Some one being asked as to a monument to mark his last resting place said, 'Let me live in the hearts of my people. I ask for no other monument.' We believe that our departed brother will live in the hearts of his people. The evidences manifested at his funeral were of such a character as to show that where he was best known he was most loved. Strong men wept as they took a last look at his familiar face and the members of the church at North Manchester and surrounding congregations showed that they felt they had lost a faithful shepherd and a kind, loving father.

"Brother Miller's death is not simply a local loss. His influence and labor were not circumscribed by the lines of a local congregation, or by the bounds of a State District. His influence was felt over our entire Brotherhood, and his place in our Annual Conference, as a wise counselor and a faithful adherent to the principles of the church, will not soon be filled. He was a man who had the courage of his convictions and manfully maintained them. He loved the church of his choice, and her principles were dear to his heart. He was a true champion and a defender of the faith. He gave the best years of his life to her service and died in the full vigor of ripening age. The last sermon he preached was marked by all the force and power which he knew so well how to use. He spoke over an hour and held the interest of his large audience to the very close. Some of us, who have heard him often, felt that it was one of his best efforts. His life was a grand success, not as the world counts success, for he had but little of this world's goods, but in abundant and far-reaching labor for the church of God.

"For some years we have been intimately associated with him in our work. As we came to know him well, our love for him as a man and a brother and our respect for his abilities and faithfulness to the church increased. He was a man you could depend upon and you could always tell where to find him. The church was always first with him and to her interests he was true, first, last and all the time. He was a warm-hearted friend, and to those who knew him well there was a depth of love and earnestness unknown to the casual observer. He had a kind heart, and to us he often spoke kindly of those who had gone away from the church, and no one regretted more than he the causes which led to the final rupture. When it came he stood unflinchingly by the church and defended her with all the rare ability with which God had endowed him. But he has gone. The church has lost one of her pillars and those who know him best, a warm-hearted, loving brother and friend. May not his life of faithfulness be helpful to us? May it not prove an incentive to us all to be faithful unto death?

"The story of his life of labor and love is written in the hearts of the people for whom he labored, but it should be written on paper and published for the encouragement of others, and we hope some one will undertake this labor of love."

In March, 1893, the *Phrenological Journal,* published by Fowler and Wells, New York, contained a well executed picture of Brother Robert, with a carefully prepared delineation of his character by Prof. Sizer, one of the most noted phrenologists in the world. There are, no doubt, many of our readers who do not believe in phrenological characterizations, but we insert this one, believing that it will be of interest to all. Many of the traits spoken of will be recognized as true of the subject.

"The photograph of this man indicates mental and physical activity, with a combination of fineness of quality, endurance and force. In any field of endeavor he would have been, in his way, a master. Had he been a seaman he would have wanted half a gale of wind to sail in; he would not have been satisfied with a ten-knot breeze. Had he been engaged in railroading, he would have wanted the lightning express. Had he held the reins of the road, he would have wanted a brisk team and a clear path. His whole constitution glows with life, vim and vigor; and while he has force that belongs to the masculine nature, the mandatory enthusiasm that seeks to master whatever opposes and needs to be conformed and reformed, he has the sensitive instincts of the feminine, which make him a sharp critic, a clear-cut thinker, and a man of wonderful power to make definite the thought he wishes to express. We judge therefore, that the front part of his head, the intellectual, the perceptive, and the intuitive elements were inherited from his mother. He thinks as she thought, he knows as she knew; he appreciates as the head that belongs to the masculine, the father. That gives him the earnest energy and the commanding spirit which wields an influence and moves powerfully wherever these things act.

"He has large cautiousness; the head is broad at the upper back corner, upward and backward from the ears; that enables him to sound the alarm. He would have been a good pioneer; a good leader of men as a soldier; and a natural herald of truth which he deemed important. He has large consciousness that gives him a sense of righteousness, a feeling of justice and judgment. He is a natural John the Baptist, whose message was: 'Prepare ye the way of the Lord, make his paths straight. Repent for the kingdom of heaven is at hand.'

"He has large firmness, which gives him determination; and that is seen in every feature of his face, decision and earnestness. It is seen in the organ of firmness, in the center of the back part of the top of his head. His veneration gives him a sense of divine right, power and worth. His benevolence renders him sympathetic toward those he wishes to serve. He has the enthusiasm which comes from ideality and sublimity, hence he would be eloquent in a cause he adopted and believed. He has discrimination and criticism, knowledge of character, power to impress his thought upon others partly because he is in magnetic touch with other people and because he has an instinct to understand the character of those whom he meets.

"Another of the traits shown in the portrait is order. He is systematic, critical, in earnest and honest; and all these conditions are fortified by courage and fear; courage to meet opposition and fear for the danger he is trying to protect himself and others against. He has a good memory, what he knows is at his command. He has fluency of speech but its peculiarity is rather the crispness and grit which his words have, in burning where he scathes, and melting where his tenderness is brought to bear. He would tell a pathetic story so as to bring tears to every eye. He would scathe rampant unrighteousness in a way to make sinners tremble. If he were prosecuting attorney in civil court he would make a man feel what a monster of wickedness he was, as Warren Hastings said he did when Burke was scathing him in his famous trial.

"Hastings said the only relief he had under the scathing was the consciousness that he had not violated his conscience. If this man were a prosecuting attorney, if a man were guilty he would make him seem as guilty as he was; he would make him feel like confessing and throwing himself on the mercy of the court. There are some mental constitutions which, when exercised upon the outward life, produce a sedative effect, the diction is smooth, the thoughts lacking in pungency and the effect is like the polishing process in mechanics. When a constitution like this is on fire, the results are specific as the path of the glazier's diamond that makes a mark on the glass to facilitate its separation. The diamond cuts in one place and a jar brings the pane of glass apart.

"His manner may at times have in it the flavor of severity, because his mind is so clear and his conclusions so sharp, backed up and pushed with such earnestness that the guilty feel guilty when he reproves, and the righteous rejoice when he commends. He would have made his mark in any field of effort. He would have been a fine mechanic, a good artist, an excellent chemist; scholar; physician; a successful teacher; and yet in his easy hours he is able to say bright, generous and gentle things that awaken toward him affection and familiar respect."

Two more characterizations of Brother Robert by brethren who knew him well will suffice to impress the reader with the genuine worth of the man. The first is by Brother W. R. Deeter, whose associations with him were such that he is in a position to speak truly:

"It was my privilege to be associated with Brother Miller in different kinds of church work; so we learned to know something of this distinguished brother. One feature that was prominent in his makeup was that he had the courage to carry out his convictions, though they might not be popular. The only question with him was, What is right and what is best? That settled all with him. He had the wisdom to know when to speak and how to speak to make his work effectual. In debate he was deliberate, rarely, if ever, losing himself. His antagonist had to be well fortified to be able to meet his forcible arguments. Truth in his hands lost nothing. He acquitted himself heroically and humbly, and vindicated the principles of the church successfully. He loved the church of which he was a member and no sacrifice was too great for him to make in vindication of her principles.

"His counsel was often sought by his brethren when hard problems were to be met; so well was he posted on church government, that he was able to give advice for the settlement of the most difficult problems. In the pulpit he was able, forcible, logical and fearless. His language was good, yet so common that the most illiterate could understand him. His social qualities were commendable, always willing to speak to and listen to all honorable classes. He was very severe in reproof when he thought it necessary. I have seen strong men wilt under his severe rebukes."

Elder Enoch Eby also speaks of his former colaborer as follows: " I was often permitted to work with him on different lines of church work, and I never found a more reliable brother in all that he was asked to do. He was an intellectual giant, especially in defending the truths of the Bible. His Christian character was unimpeachable; he always manifested a dignified humility. He was an able defender of our church policy against all opposition. I never was about a man I could take into my confidence more than he. Finally, if I had been required to get a man possessing all the qualifications of Christian usefulness that can be found in human nature, and that can be used in any department of church work as a power for good, I would have laid my hands on the shoulders of Brother R. H. Miller, and said ' Here is the man.' "

## CHAPTER XI.

### Contemporaries.

During his lifetime, Brother Robert Miller was associated with men of noble character and great ability. With many of these he labored long and faithfully for the welfare of the church. If the history of all their labors could be written, it would form an interesting and instructive volume. But the silent past has forever sealed the story of much of their lives. Their unselfish deeds will form a part of that great volume of the unwritten history of uncrowned heroes.

For the instruction and encouragement of our young members, brief sketches are here given of a few of these men. The list is far from complete and but few facts are recorded in each. This is partly because it is not desirable to extend this volume and partly because of a lack of knowledge concerning the lives of these brethren. The first four biographies given are of men with whom Brother Robert was but little associated but who evidently had their influence on his life. Then there are leaders in the church today who knew him well and often labored with him. Their biographies have been left for the future historian to record. Many of them have kindly contributed to this volume by giving desired information, or by expressing their estimate of Brother Robert's characteristics.

### ELDER GEORGE WOLFE.

Elder George Wolfe was born in Lancaster County, Pa., April 25, 1780. His father, Elder George Wolfe, crossed the Alleghany Mountains to western Pennsylvania in 1787, and after thirteen years of labor there he moved his family to Kentucky, where he continued to reside until 1809, when he died on his homeward journey from an extensive preaching tour in Missouri and Illinois. George Wolfe, Jr., was married in Kentucky in 1803 and in 1808, accompanied by his brother, he moved to southwestern Illinois. In 1812 he and thirteen of his friends and neighbors were baptized by Elder John Hendricks, of Kentucky. In the same year Brother Wolfe was called to the ministry, and the next year ordained to the eldership. Then for more than fifty years, he was an untiring worker among the pioneers and was the chief factor in the establishment of many churches. He possessed marvelous natural ability, an eloquent pulpit orator, a profound reasoner in debate and discourse, a constant reader who acquired a vast amount of knowledge, and a Christian whose integrity was never questioned.

He did not attend the Annual Meetings and so did not influence directly the decisions of that body; but indirectly he did. The Far Western Brethren, as Elder Wolfe and his followers were known to the East, practiced the single mode of feet-washing, had no intermission between the Lord's supper and the communion service, and allowed the sisters to break the bread and pass the cup the same as the brethren. In 1856 he had a long conference with a committee from Annual Meeting and agreed "to conform to the practice of the brethren in general, when in communion meeting with them and begged forbearance on the part of the brethren in general until they all should come to see alike." This forbearance was granted, but the conviction gradually took hold of the eastern brethren that the single mode of feet-washing, as practiced by the western brethren, was right, and the practice spread until it has become the general order of the church. Elder George Wolfe died in 1865, at the ripe old age of eighty-five.

### ELDER JOHN KLINE.

Elder John Kline was born in Rockingham County, Va., June 17, 1797. He never went to school very much but learned to read and write both English and German. After his marriage he lived on a farm near the place of his birth; but in time he also became a practicing physician. He was elected to the ministry about 1834 and preached his first sermon Feb. 8, 1835. At this time he began keeping a diary, and continued to do so for twenty-nine years. These records, which have been published in book form by his old friend, Benjamin Funk, tell of his many visits in Virginia and other States. They also record synopses of many of the sermons delivered by himself and other brethren. He has left an account of many visits to families in Virginia and included many items of their family history. He served on the Standing Committee nearly every year for twenty years, and was moderator the last four years of his life. He was fully alive to the missionary work in the church. His yearly travels were very great, amounting to as much as 6,500 miles in a single year. He generally went on horseback and his diary gives much credit to faithful Nell. Often he would have appointments for preaching every day for weeks ahead. He was faithful to every trust committed to him and never disappointed his people. He had a commanding presence, a wonderful knowledge of the Scriptures and a power to deliver his messages in an effective way. His advice was much sought on matters pertaining to the welfare of the church. In some years he preached as many as fifty funerals.

He opposed slavery, war and secession. In this way he incurred the hatred of the enemies of his country. After the great rebellion began he continued to pass through the lines to visit his northern brethren. In the spring of 1864 he attended the Annual Meeting at Hagerstown, Ind., and took a prominent part. He preached at many places on this journey. He fully realized his danger in his valley home, but he returned with the faith that whatever might happen all was well. On June 15, 1864, he went a short distance from home to get Nell shod. Later in the day he was found dead by the roadside, his body pierced by several bullets. It is said that the assassins later met unhappy fates, but the first martyr missionary of the Church of the Brethren in America rested in the embrace of death, with a heavenly smile upon his countenance. By tender hands his loving remains were laid to rest in the Linville cemetery, where a simple marble slab now marks the grave of this saintly herald of the cross.

### ELDER PETER NEAD.

Elder Peter Nead was born in Hagerstown, Md., Jan. 7, 1796. He received a good education for his day. His grandfather, who was a Lutheran, as were also his parents, wanted to educate young Peter for a Lutheran preacher. He declined the offer and later learned the trade of a tanner. About this time he became interested in his soul's welfare. He first joined the Methodists and became a class leader and a preacher among them. He was not satisfied, however, with his fraternity and for a while became an independent preacher. Then happening to read a pamphlet written by one of the Brethren he became interested in their doctrine. A visit to a communion service further convinced him that the Brethren's position was right. He at once joined the church and was soon put to the ministry. His ability to preach in English caused his services to be in demand. He married Elizabeth Yount, of Rockingham County, Va., in 1825. He taught school and conducted a tanning business, while at the same time he was becoming more actively engaged in his ministerial work. In 1840 he moved to Augusta County, Va., and three years later to Botetourt

County. In 1850 he located in the Lower Stillwater church near Dayton, Ohio, where he continued to reside till his death, which occurred March 16, 1877.

Elder Nead was one of the most active writers of the church in his day. In 1833 he wrote a work entitled "Primitive Christianity," which treated of the ordinances and doctrines of the church. The work, which contained 138 pages, was much read. In 1845 he wrote another book of about the same size on baptism and other subjects. These two books were combined into one volume, and with some additional writing were published as "Nead's Theology" in 1850. This book became a standard work in the church. His last book, written in 1866, was entitled "Wisdom and Power of God as Displayed in Creation and Redemption." A little later he assisted in starting the new church periodical, the *Vindicator*. Through this he strongly opposed the changes that were taking place in the church.

From his first acquaintance with the Brethren, he always loved their principles and customs. His main purpose in life was the welfare and purity of the church. He was a diligent student of the Bible, an edifying preacher and a safe man in counsel. He served on the Standing Committee quite a number of times. He was fearless in defending the truth as he saw it. He was a faithful shepherd to his home congregation and gave much assistance to surrounding churches. His health remained good almost to the last, though he died at the ripe old age of eighty-one. By request he was buried in a plain coffin before the funeral service, "For why," said he, "should the dead body be taken to the meetinghouse? It can't hear." No one was especially selected to preach but the brethren present improved the occasion.

### ELDER HENRY KURTZ.

Elder Henry Kurtz was born in Germany, July 22, 1796. He received a very good education, intending to follow the profession of teaching. Later he prepared for the Lutheran ministry. He came to America in 1819. While on his voyage he became acquainted with a young man who had been educated for a Catholic priest. Years afterward these two men met at an Annual Meeting, not a Lutheran and Catholic, but both of them ministers of the Church of the Brethren. Upon his arrival he at once entered upon his ministerial duties in Northampton County, Pa. The next year he married Anna Catherine Loehr. Three years later he moved to Pittsburg, where he remained three years. While engaged in his work here he began to doubt the validity of infant baptism. When he made known his conviction quite a stir was made by the Lutherans. He was finally excommunicated and lost his charge. In 1826 he moved to Ohio and settled in Stark County the next spring. He had learned of the Brethren and soon became much interested in their faith and practice. He was baptized in 1828 and elected to the ministry two years later. His father-in-law opposed his joining the church. He persuaded a schoolteacher, Frederick P. Loehr, to try to convince Henry that the Brethren were not right. Loehr failed in his mission and later he himself was baptized and became an elder in the church.

In 1838 Elder Kurtz returned to Germany on a visit to his parents. While here he preached in Switzerland and baptized several members. He continued to reside in Stark County until 1842, when he was called to the Mill Creek church, Mahoning County. Here he was ordained to the eldership in 1844. He was elder of this congregation for thirty years. His fine education made him a very useful man in the church; especially in the Annual Meeting, where he served on the Standing Committee twenty times, acting as clerk nearly every year. In 1851 he revived the literary activity of the church by sending out the first numbers of the *Gospel Visitor*. For ten years he had desired to do something of this kind, but the brethren had never considered it advisable. His early trials were severe and the life of his paper uncertain. Finally the Annual Meeting refused to interfere and the paper became firmly established. In 1856 he secured as his assistant James Quinter, who became editor when Elder Kurtz retired in 1864. He used German fluently and preferred to write his editorials in his native tongue and have them translated into English. He was wide-awake on the question of higher education. He possessed much musical ability, both vocal and instrumental. He was one of only a very few Brethren who possessed an organ in those days. As his ability was more along literary and editorial lines, he did not become active in committee work. He died on Jan. 12, 1874, aged 77 years, 5 months and 21 days.

### ELDER H. D. DAVY.

For twelve consecutive years, after the death of Elder John Kline, Elder Henry D. Davy of Miami County, Ohio, successfully presided over the Annual Meeting as its moderator. For this work he seems to have been preëminently fitted. He had never received much of an education, but his ability in the pulpit was far above the average minister of his day. He made very little pretense along literary lines. He was much in demand as a committeeman to help settle church difficulties. In this work he was often associated with Elder R. H. Miller. In 1876 he and Elder James Quinter collected in book form the Minutes of Annual Meeting up to that time. Later, when the division came, he cast his lot with the Old Order Brethren. He was prominent in their annual councils, of which he was moderator for several years. He died Sept. 7, 1895, at the age of eighty-four years.

### ELDER B. F. MOOMAW.

Elder Benjamin F. Moomaw was born March 30, 1813, and died at his home near Bonsacks, Va., Nov. 6, 1900, in his eighty-eighth year. His education was limited, and yet it was fairly good for his day. But through a long life of service and study he became widely known all over the Brotherhood as an author and preacher of great ability. He was elected to the ministry and ordained to the eldership while yet a young man. He became the owner of a large farm and was very successful in all his business transactions. Here in his commodious, picturesque, southern home he entertained hundreds of brethren who always enjoyed his hospitality and the charm of his extraordinary conversational powers. He built up a large congregation over which he presided with rare skill and firmness. He was cool and level-headed in all circumstances in life. Like Elder John Kline, he opposed slavery, secession and war. His life was in much danger during the rebellion, but he so conducted himself that after the conflict was over he had the respect of both parties. He was instrumental in getting the Confederate Congress to exempt the Brethren from military duty on payment of five hundred dollars.

He was prominent in the Annual Meeting, serving on the Standing Committee seven times. He served on some of the most important committees ever appointed by Annual Meeting. In later years he was familiarly known everywhere as "Father Moomaw." He wrote much for the church periodicals on various subjects. He once held a debate by letter with a Rev. Jackson, on the subject of baptism. In this debate he had the unusual success of converting his opponent and baptizing him into the Church of the Brethren. Another one of his books, "The Divinity of Christ," grew out of the question, "What Think Ye of Christ?" put to him

# CONTEMPORARIES

by a young man who could not accept the divinity of Christ. He devoted his last hours to reminiscences of his church work and telling of the blessings with which God had crowned his days. He told his family that he was going to the grave with the same satisfaction that he went to hear a sermon on a pleasant day.

### ELDER JOHN METZGER.

Elder John Metzger was born in Blair County, Pa., Dec. 20, 1807. His grandparents had emigrated from Holland to Baltimore in 1758, where each was sold for several years' service to pay for their passage across the Atlantic. When John was twelve years old his parents moved to Dayton, Ohio. Here he married Hannah Ulrey, in 1828, and soon after this both of them joined the Church of the Brethren. In 1834 they moved to Tippecanoe County, Ind., where he was elected to the ministry in the next year. He saw that the harvest was great but the laborers indeed were few. He preached his first sermon in a sawmill. He had varied experiences in preaching to the hardy pioneers, but the Lord blessed his work and many were brought into the church.

He was ordained to the eldership in 1843. After 1848 he seldom missed an Annual Meeting, always paying his own expenses and preaching at many places, both going and coming. About 1860 he moved to Cerro Gordo, Ill. He called upon Abraham Lincoln at Springfield just before the President-elect started for Washington. He continued his ministerial work in his new home with unabated zeal and often went back to his old Indiana home, preaching at many places along the way. It is said that he preached in at least twenty different States. Through his efforts many members were brought to the church in St. Louis.

Though he started poor in life, and always sacrificed his own interests to those of the church, yet the Lord blessed him in temporal things, a due part of which he returned to the Giver. In 1878 he built a house of worship at Cerro Gordo, Ill. Elder R. H. Miller dedicated it to the service of God.

In 1887 his aged wife died and two years later he married sister Parmelia Wolfe, the widowed daughter-in-law of Elder George Wolfe. In 1890 they moved to Lordsburg, Cal. Here he spent his last years peacefully. He engaged in planting a fruit orchard and was interested in the Lordsburg College. He gave his last address at the district meeting of California, in March, 1896. Shortly after this he made one more journey across the Rocky Mountains, to his old home at Cerro Gordo. Here on May 25, 1896, surrounded by his family, he peacefully fell asleep. Thus ended the noble life of one who had served the church for sixty-one years in the ministry, had been on eighteen Standing Committees, had acted on dozens of committees sent to all parts of the Brotherhood and had traveled thousands of miles to tell the sweet story of the cross. By his unselfish labors hundreds had been brought into the fold of Jesus Christ.

### ELDER D. P. SAYLOR.

Elder Daniel P. Saylor was born near Beaver Dam, Frederick County, Md., June 23, 1811. His great-grandfather, Daniel P., was a native of Switzerland. His grandfather, Elder Daniel Saylor, and his uncle, Elder Jacob Saylor, were both able men in the church. Brother Saylor was baptized in 1837 and three years later was elected to the ministry, in the same year his grandfather died. It is said that when he was elected he became angry and said that the church evidently lacked judgment, because he was unqualified and could never preach. However, he thought the matter over seriously and through the encouragement of Elder Price, he finally accepted the work.

He was soon and very unexpectedly put to work by the old brethren insisting on his preaching the funeral of a child. From the words, "I am the resurrection and the life," he preached such an eloquent discourse that every one was astonished. The news spread rapidly and soon he had many calls for preaching in all the surrounding country. The effectiveness of his work can best be judged by the fact that in 1842, inside of three months, ninety-two persons were baptized in the Beaver Dam church and the old meetinghouse had to be enlarged.

In this year he was advanced to the second degree of the ministry and was ordained to the eldership on May 7, 1850. His work among the churches was so great that only a man of his strong physical build could have endured the stress. On horseback he made many long missionary journeys to the churches, always paying his own expenses. On these journeys he was often accompanied by Elder John H. Umstad, of Pennsylvania. Beginning in 1851 he served on the Standing Committee twenty-four times. Of that body he was frequently clerk or moderator.

Probably no man ever had a greater formative influence on the decisions of Annual Meeting than he. He was devotedly attached to the principles of the church which he understood well. This together with his wide experience enabled him to be of great service to his brethren. In 1848 he framed the questions that are still asked of applicants for baptism. In 1860 he was the chairman of a committee—Elders John Kline, James Quinter and John Metzger being the other members—that presented to Annual Meeting an excellent plan for missionary work. While it was not accepted, it was placed on the Minutes and evidently helped to arouse the missionary spirit. One paragraph of this report is worth repeating, because it recommends our present plan of having district meetings, which were adopted in 1866 on the recommendation of another committee, of which Elder Saylor was chairman; and because it recommends the weekly offering which we have not yet been willing to try!

"The committee offers the following advice: That the churches of the Brotherhood form themselves into districts to meet as often as they may judge it necessary to transact their business; that each of said districts have its treasury, and each of the churches which form said districts have its treasury, the former to be supplied by the latter, and the latter to be supplied by weekly contributions as directed by the Apostle Paul (1 Cor. 16:2): 'Upon the first day of the week let every one of you lay by him in store, as God has prospered him, that there be no gatherings when I come,'—a plan for raising pecuniary funds of divine appointment, and one which commends itself to our acceptance, both from its authority and excellency."

He served on many committees of importance like this one. It would be hard to estimate the extent of his influence. He was a close observer, a careful investigator and a fine organizer. Besides he had the natural ability and that fearless disposition that carried out what he decided to be right. Though he was very progressive in his views of missionary work, Sunday schools, education, etc., yet he had no sympathy whatever with the so-called progressive movement. It was mostly through his influence that H. R. Holsinger was not given more time at the Annual Meeting of 1882.

With him the great question was, What is right? Having decided this, neither policy nor feeling could turn him aside. This may be seen from a letter to Elder R. H. Miller, in which he upbraids Brother Robert for giving advice to a brother in Kansas to wait until Annual Meeting would give consent to receive persons living in second marriage when the cause of separation had been fornication. Brother Saylor believed that the Savior's word,

"Except it be for fornication," gave full privilege to the innocent party to marry again. "Brother Miller well knows that Brother Saylor is a strong advocate of the decisions of Annual Meeting on all questions on which the Scriptures are silent. But as soon as Annual Meeting will assume the authority to decide a question contrary to the expressed word of the Lord I am and will be her bitter opponent, and will never submit to a decision contrary to the expressed word of the Lord."—*Primitive Christian, June 1, 1880.*

He was a frequent contributor to the church papers. He was one of the associate editors of the *Pilgrim.* He was ever a strong opponent of slavery. The Union men of Maryland desired to make him a member of the constitutional convention in 1864, but he refused. Though he spent much time for the church, yet he prospered financially. He never wanted to be burdensome to his brethren. He always paid his own way to Annual Meeting, whether delegate or not. He was twice married. His first wife died in 1874. His second wife and a young babe survived his death, which occurred June 6, 1885. His last illness of heart trouble and dropsy was partly brought on by exposure while holding a series of meetings. He always enjoyed life, and while he endured his sufferings patiently and was perfectly resigned to go, yet, if it had been his Lord's will, he would have cheerfully borne the cross longer.

After his death, his colaborer, Elder James Quinter, who knew him so well, characterized him as follows: "He and I entered the ministry at nearly the same time, and we labored together in the church to which we were both warmly attached, nearly half a century. We were intimately acquainted with one another and the bonds of brotherly love united us closely together. We often in our church labors wept together over the troubles of our beloved Zion, but also often rejoiced together in the joy of the Holy Spirit. Brother Saylor was a man of prayer and of deep experience in the ways and workings of the Holy Spirit."

### ELDER JAMES QUINTER.

Elder James Quinter was born in Philadelphia, Feb. 1, 1816. The father was a daily laborer, and in 1826 he moved his family to Phoenixville, Pa., where he worked in the iron mills. Three years later he died, leaving the burden of supporting his family upon his thirteen-year-old son, James. This interfered with the boy's school privileges, but he attended school as much as possible. The course of study was not extensive, but it was enriched by plenty of selections from standard authors, and above all by the study of the Bible, which inspired the youthful student to higher things in life.

After leaving school he worked for a time in the store of Brother Isaac Price. Later he went to live on the farm in the home of Brother Abel Fitzwater. Through the influence of this Christian family and of other brethren in the neighborhood he was converted and baptized about 1832. From the first he was very zealous and devoted in his religious duties. Protracted meetings and prayer meetings gave much spiritual food to his hungry soul.

His thirst for knowledge also increased. By private study and by spending some time in a private school, he was able to begin teaching school, first, near Royer's Ford, and later at Lumberville, Pa., where he continued to work from 1834 till 1841. In 1838 he was called to the ministry, a work to which he had long felt that he had been set apart by God. His deep religious life and his many intellectual attainments, the result of constant study and self culture, at once brought him in favor with the Brethren. The next year he accompanied Brother John Umstad on a preaching tour through Pennsylvania. His services were also much sought in the neighboring States of New Jersey and Maryland. In 1842 he responded to a call from the George's Creek church, Fayette County, Pa. Here his ministry was blessed with wonderful results. About sixty persons were baptized here during the first six months of his labors. Among them was John Wise, who later became Brother Quinter's great colaborer in the church.

The church in Fayette County presented him with a small farm. To this be brought his mother, his widowed sister and her three boys. In 1850 he married Mary Ann Moser, who died of consumption seven years later, leaving a daughter, Lydia Isabella. He taught school for a number of winters and for a time examined the teachers of his township as to their fitness for teaching.

At the Annual Meeting in 1855 he was appointed

## CONTEMPORARIES

assistant to Elder Henry Kurtz, who had for years been writing clerk. He performed his work to the satisfaction of all. Elder Kurtz had been wanting a suitable brother to aid him on the *Gospel Visitor.* He now felt that God had pointed out Brother James Quinter. The latter responded to the call and moved to Poland, Mahoning County, Ohio, in 1856. His parting from those he had labored with so long was not without pain; but he felt the call to broader fields of service.

In 1857 the office of the *Gospel Visitor* was moved to Columbiana, Ohio. He showed ability as an editor. He also began to take an interest in higher education in the church. A school had been planned at Columbiana, but due consideration showed him that it would not be advisable. Later the opportunity opened up favorably at New Vienna, Ohio. Here a school was opened in 1861. It continued three years, when it had to be closed on account of the disturbances resulting from the Civil War. In the same year Elder Henry Kurtz retired from active work and Brother Quinter became chief editor of the *Gospel Visitor.* In 1866 the office was moved to Covington, Ohio. In 1874 he purchased the entire interests of the *Visitor* and also the *Christian Family Companion* and consolidated them, retaining both names on the new paper. This was published at Myersdale, Pa., to which State he returned after nearly twenty years' residence in Ohio. In 1876 he again consolidated his paper with the *Pilgrim,* published by the Brumbaugh Bros. at Huntingdon, Pa. Here he became chief editor of the new paper, the *Primitive Christian*. In 1883 this paper and the *Brethren at Work* were consolidated under the name of *Gospel Messenger*, of which Brother Quinter remained editor-in-chief until his death.

During this time he also was wielding an influence for higher education in the church. His first attempts had not resulted in what he expected, though through no fault of his own. In 1879 Prof. J. M. Zuck, the founder of Huntingdon Normal, died. The trustees at once elected Brother Quinter president, a position which he held the rest of his life.

However active he was along these intellectual lines, he was just as active in church work. He was ordained to the eldership in 1856. For thirty successive years, except one, he was a member of the Standing Committee—the longest service ever given by one man on that body. His attainments made him the only choice of the brethren for writing clerk. During these years he was sent on dozens of committees to all parts of the Brotherhood. There were but very few important committees of which he was not a member. His great ability made him the only choice of his brethren in defending the principles of the church in public debate until R. H. Miller took up that work. He had no particular liking for this work, but felt it his duty to respond to the call. His earnest, dignified, Christian spirit, as well as his ability in the Bible and in knowledge of history, made him a strong defender of the truth.

He had few equals in the pulpit. His sermons were well prepared and delivered in the power of the Holy Spirit. Many of them have been preserved and edited, together with a history of his life, by his daughter, Mary A. Quinter. Seldom did he pass a Sunday without preaching. His sermons were addressed to the intelligence as well as to the heart. He was especially influential with people of superior culture.

It would be impossible to estimate the result of his thirty-two years of constant editorial service. His opinion and advice on church doctrine and difficult questions were often sought and as freely given. Whether men agreed with him or not, one thing is certain, they always respected him and never doubted his sincerity. Besides his printed debates and sermons, he has left an extended work on baptism, the best exposition of the subject in the literature of the church.

His name was familiar wherever his brethren lived. When a boy, the writer well remembers his desire to attend the Annual Meeting at North Manchester, Ind., 1888, that he might hear Elder James Quinter preach. Hundreds of others went to that meeting with the same desire. He was to preach in the tabernacle on Sunday morning. But the Lord knoweth best. On Saturday Brother Quinter arrived on the grounds. In the afternoon he listened to a sermon by Elder Daniel Vaniman. He closed the services by a few fitting remarks and hymn and then called to prayer. While thus engaged in pouring out his heart to God the heavenly messenger gave him the welcome to come home, and amid the tears and sobs of a large audience and the tender ministrations of loving hands, his spirit took its flight. After a few appropriate and touching remarks by Elder Enoch Eby, the remains were prepared for the solemn journey to his home in Huntingdon, where he was laid to rest. He left three daughters, the two younger, Mary and Grace, being the children of a second marriage to Fannie Studebaker, who also survived him. Mary is the author and editor of "Life and Sermons of Elder James Quinter." For several years she has been one of our faithful missionaries in India. His oldest daughter, Lydia, became the wife of Elder J. T. Myers in 1877.

This brief biography can in no way do justice to one whose life was so full of service and blessings to his fellows. His labors are written in the history of the church, his memory is still dear in the hearts of all who knew him and his name is in the Lamb's Book of Life over yonder. Space forbids further comment on his character, but it may be summed up by saying that he was a man, a Christian man in the fullest sense of the word.

D. P. Saylor, James Quinter, R. H. Miller: These three formed a triumvirate that worked together in harmony. They were not alike in character; rather their powers were complementary. For years they were the leaders of the church that they loved. Their equals would be hard to find. Their lives of devotion and service are worthy of imitation by any minister of the Gospel.

### ELDER ENOCH EBY.

Elder Enoch Eby was born in Juniata County, Pa., Nov. 15, 1828. He united with the church in 1845, and six years later was called to the ministry. In 1847 he married Hetty Howe. He acquired sufficient education to enable him to teach school in the winter and farm in the summer. He entered the work of the ministry with a spirit to do what he could.

In 1855 he moved his family to Stephenson County, Ill. Here he was the means of bringing many into the church. He was ordained in 1864, and at once took charge of the church. His wife died in 1867 and several of his children within a few years following. All of his children united with the church when they were young. In 1870 he married Anna (Lauver) Gilfilen, of Perry County, Pa.

Brother Eby was closely associated with the early missionary efforts in the church. It came about in this way: In 1870 two Baptist ministers, Christian Hope and Christian Hansen, came from Denmark to the United States. They had, however, severed their former church relations because they believed their mode of baptism to be wrong. Christian Hansen soon returned to Denmark, but Christian Hope remained here until he found the Brethren and accepted their teaching. He was baptized in the Hickory Grove congregation of Northern Illinois, Oct. 25, 1874.

Brother Hope at once felt an interest in his friends at home and desired the brethren to send a minister to them. Christian Hansen, then in Denmark, who had read tracts sent by the Brethren, also earnestly appealed for a minister who would preach the whole Gospel. The elders of Northern Illinois heard the Macedonian call and acted promptly. They elected Brother Hope to the ministry that he might go and preach to his countrymen. They also selected elders Enoch Eby and Paul Wetzel to accompany Brother Hope. They then appealed to Annual Meeting to endorse their work.

The leading men of the conference at once showed that they were thoroughly in sympathy with the movement, but did not feel to burden Annual Meeting with the expense. Brother Hope went to Denmark wholly on the support of Northern Illinois, and though he had to work hard against many obstacles, before another year his work was bearing fruit.

In 1877 a paper passed Annual Meeting, recommending the Danish Mission to the sympathy and support of the general Brotherhood. Brethren were appointed to receive contributions at that meeting. The next year the conference decided that the Danish Mission should be left in the care of Northern Illinois, but that it was the duty of the entire Brotherhood to pay the expense.

In the fall of 1877 Brother and Sister Enoch Eby and Brother and Sister Daniel Fry crossed the Atlantic on the first foreign missionary tour ever sent out by the Church of the Brethren. They reached Hjorring Denmark, where they organized a church of thirteen members. Brother C. Eskildsen was chosen minister. The next spring they returned to America, leaving Brother Hope with encouraging prospects to continue the work.

In 1880 the Annual Meeting assumed control of the Danish Mission by placing it under the care of our first recognized Mission Board. The members of this committee were James Quinter, S. T. Bosserman, Joseph Leedy, Daniel Brubaker, and Enoch Eby. Four years later this General Mission Board was superseded by the General Church Erection and Missionary Committee. Brother Eby was the only member of the first committee that served on the new one. He was its first president and served a number of terms. D. L. Miller was secretary and treasurer. The other members were C. P. Rowland, Daniel Vaniman, and Samuel Riddlesbarger. In 1894 this committee was consolidated with the Brethren's Book and Tract Committee, under the name of General Missionary and Tract Committee.

Brother Eby has lived to see this Board become the most influential committee in the church. The funds placed in its hands have grown immensely by endowments, gifts and the proceeds of the Publishing House, which came into the possession of the general Brotherhood in 1897. He has seen missions opened in Asia Minor, India, Switzerland, France, China, and in many of the largest cities of the United States. The church, which was slow to take hold of the mission work thirty years ago, is alive today with missionary zeal.

Brother Eby has been a member of the Standing Committee nineteen times. He has proved himself one of the best moderators that ever presided over Annual Meeting, having served in that capacity eleven times. He has served on many committees of importance. For several years he lived at Booth, Kans., but is now at his old home at Lena, Stephenson County, Ill.

### ELDER JOHN WISE.

Elder John Wise was born in western Pennsylvania in 1822. He received a good education in his youth. He began teaching when he was eighteen and taught about thirty terms in Pennsylvania and Texas. He was baptized June 14, 1842, under the preaching of Elder James Quinter. He was elected to the ministry the next year. During his early ministry he was often associated with Brother Quinter, to whom he looked for advice as a son would to his father. He was ordained to the eldership in 1854.

Brother Wise was small of stature, yet he possessed a remarkable voice. This, together with his good education and great knowledge of the Scriptures, caused his services to be useful to the church in many ways. He was probably the best reading clerk that ever served the Annual Meeting. He was reading clerk fifteen times and moderator in 1885. He served on many important committees, including the Berlin Committee, that disfellowshiped H. R. Holsinger in 1881, and the committee on the divorce question, 1888-1891, in which he made a firm stand against the position of Elder R. H. Miller.

He was a very forceful speaker in the pulpit. His travels were very extensive, amounting to as much as fifteen thousand miles in one year. In 1881 he, in company with Brother David Ruple, spent forty days among the River Brethren of Canada. They were considering the advisability of a union between the River Brethren and the Church of the Brethren. The visit was a pleasant one, though the union was never brought about. About thirty years ago he moved from Pennsylvania to Iowa, and later on to Kansas, where he died June 26, 1909, at the age of eighty-seven years, having served in the ministry two-thirds of a century. Several years before his death he lost his sight, but had partially regained it before his death.

### ELDER JAMES R. GISH.

Elder James R. Gish was born in Roanoke County, Va., in 1824. His parents, who were members of the Brethren church, set before him examples of righteous living. He was in poor circumstances and had to work hard when a boy. He received very little education; but by his careful study of the Scriptures he later became a minister of ability.

He was married to Barbara Kindig in 1849. In the same year they emigrated to Woodford County, Ill., where they secured some excellent land at a very low price. They united with the church in 1852, and Brother Gish was elected to the ministry in the same year. His sterling character gave great power to his preaching. He knew the Scriptures well and had the fearless disposition to expound the truth. His wife, who was a good singer and a loving woman, was of great assistance to him.

In 1854 they returned to Virginia by private conveyance. The trip occupied many weeks, but it was well spent in preaching at many places. His interest for the welfare of the church was such that he went on many missionary tours, always at his own expense. After the war he went as far south as New Orleans. Later he and his wife went on extensive journeys through Tennessee. His special concern was for the isolated places. Frequently he assisted poor ministers to locate permanently in weak churches. He was the means of building up and organizing several congregations. He preached in no less than twenty-two States. The last nine years of his life were spent in the mission fields of Arkansas. Here his labors and sacrifices were great. It is surely an encouraging picture to see this old veteran of threescore and ten, accompanied by his faithful wife, toiling in the harvest fields for the Master. Declining years did not check his activity and he passed away on the field of battle. After an illness of four months he died at Stuttgart, Ark., April 30, 1896. He was buried with his kindred and friends at Roanoke, Ill.

Notwithstanding his busy life spent for the church, Brother Gish acquired considerable means. This he used freely to aid the poor and spread the

Gospel. After his death, his generous wife turned over nearly $60,000 to the General Missionary and Tract Committee. This is known as the Gish Fund. The income is used to furnish useful books, at a nominal cost, to the ministers of the Church of the Brethren. It has, no doubt, been a great blessing to the church and will continue to be so for years to come.

### ELDER S. S. MOHLER.

Elder S. S. Mohler was born near Covington, Ohio, Sept. 22, 1832, died Dec. 4, 1893. His father, Samuel Mohler, became a most efficient elder. His mother was a relative of Elder D. P. Saylor. He received the education of the ordinary country boy of his day. He read widely and stored up many facts. In 1853 he married Mary A. Deeter, who proved an encouraging helpmeet in his ministerial work of later years. About 1857 he and his father were elected to the ministry on the same day. He was ordained Oct. 8, 1870.

He had advanced ideas on many subjects, such as missionary work, series of meetings, and Sunday schools. Finding himself opposed by brethren in Ohio, he felt the need of changing location. On invitation of Elder John Harshey, he moved to Missouri in 1869. In later years when Elder Harshey went with the Old Order Brethren, Brother Mohler became presiding bishop of the Mineral Creek congregation. He was thoroughly in sympathy with conservative methods, resisting alike the radical views of both divisions that left the church.

His belief in series of meetings caused him to do much of this kind of work in the frontier churches at a great sacrifice. He was very influential in his State district. He presided over several different congregations with great success. He did not think it best for a non-resident elder to be in charge of a congregation except when necessary. His plan was to select some suitable man for his successor and train him up to the work. For years he was prominent in our Annual Meetings, serving on the Standing Committee a number of times and acting as moderator in 1889. He did much committee work, for which he was especially adapted. It was because of his extensive service for the church that his health finally broke and a premature death resulted. His life's motto was to follow that which he believed to be right and trust to the Lord for results.

Besides being an able and much appreciated contributor to the various publications, he has performed a work that has been of great service to the church. There had been much confusion because the Minutes of Annual Meeting were not in a shape for brethren to find what the decisions were. In 1867 Elder Henry Kurtz published the Brethren's Encyclopedia, containing the Minutes then collected, In 1876 Elders H. D. Davy and James Quinter collected in chronological order the Minutes up to that date. As they were not classified, the exact minute wanted was difficult to find. In 1882 a committee of fifteen able brethren were selected to revise the Minutes and report their work to the conference.

After two years of labor and much expense the committee presented the result of their work, but it was rejected.

In the meantime Brother Mohler, who was a member of the original committee, had been classifying all the Minutes of previous years according to their respective contents. He had included all Minutes, both obsolete and those in force. When the revised Minutes failed to meet the approval of the conference, a request was made to permit the publication of Brother Mohler's work. This was at once granted. The book has proved of great value to elders as well as a source of much important historical material.

Brother Mohler's family consisted of seven sons and three daughters. All of them joined the church when young. One son died at the age of twenty-one. Another was elected to the deacon's office. The other five were elected to the ministry and have carried forward the work so nobly begun by the father. One of them, Elder Levi D. Mohler, of McPherson, died in 1908.

### ELDER DANIEL VANIMAN.

Elder Daniel Vaniman was born in Montgomery County, Ohio, Feb. 4, 1835. He was raised on a farm and did not have many educational advantages; yet by careful study, he acquired sufficient knowledge to teach school. Not content with a knowledge of common school subjects, he continued his study in higher branches until he became a man of wide learning. He had a feeling when young, that he would sometime be elected to the ministry, and quietly made preparation for the important work that was placed upon him in 1865. At this time he lived in Macoupin County, Ill. In 1876 he was ordained to the eldership and soon became a leader in southern Illinois, and well known all over the Brotherhod.

He was an enthusiastic advocate of missionary work and better methods for work at home. He was for several years a member of the Book and Tract Committee, which was organized in 1885 and consolidated with the General Church Erection and Missionary Committee in 1894. It did a great work in spreading the Gospel through the means of distributing tracts and books. He helped to originate and formulate some of our best plans for missionary work. He was foreman of many important committees, one of which proposed the present plan of holding our Annual Meetings. For several years he was the traveling secretary for the General Mission Board, and raised thousands of dollars of endowment. In this work he visited the churches in all parts of the United States.

Brother Vaniman served several times on the Standing Committee. He was moderator of the Conference three times. In characterizing his ability Elder D. L. Miller says: " He was a man with the remarkable gift of saying more in a few words than any public speaker or writer I ever knew. At Hagerstown, Md., he revolutionized the manner of presiding at our Conferences. He taught the lesson,

## CONTEMPORARIES 269

not since forgotten, that the business of a moderator is not speech-making, but giving his full attention to looking after the Conference. He was a man of system and methods, and did not fail to use them. He wrote the 'Plan for general Mission Work,' adopted by the Conference, and to him more than to any other member of the board is due the credit of opening up the India Mission Field."

Brother Vaniman was twice married. His first wife, whose maiden name was Maria Kimmel, became the mother of the late A. W. Vaniman, and soon after died of consumption. In 1861 he married Sister Stutsman, of Elkhart, Ind. She and six daughters survived his death, which occurred very suddenly at McPherson, Kans., Nov. 15, 1903. He had moved from Illinois to McPherson because he desired to enjoy an educational environment and to help build up the college.

**DATE DUE**

WITHDRAWN
from
Fondren Library